Christ All Merciful

Christ All Merciful

Megan McKenna

Icons by William Hart McNichols, S.J.

ORBIS BOOKS

Maryknoll, New York 10545

Founded in 1970, Orbis Books endeavors to publish works that enlighten the mind, nourish the spirit, and challenge the conscience. The publishing arm of the Maryknoll Fathers & Brothers, Orbis seeks to explore the global dimensions of the Christian faith and mission, to invite dialogue with diverse cultures and religious traditions, and to serve the cause of reconciliation and peace. The books published reflect the views of their authors and do not represent the official position of the Maryknoll Society. To learn more about Maryknoll and Orbis Books, please visit our website at www.maryknoll.org.

Library of Congress Cataloging-in-Publication Data

McKenna, Megan.
    Christ all merciful / Megan McKenna ; icons by William Hart McNichols.
      p. cm.
    Includes bibliographical references.
    ISBN 1-57075-449-7 (pbk.)
    1. Jesus Christ–Meditations. 2. Icons–Meditations. I. Title.
BT203 .M35 2002
232 – dc21

                                          2002004612

For Lawrence Dreffein, O.F.M.,
who first opened the door of icons for me.
May the glance of mercy remain upon you always.

MM

For Father Timothy Martinez and the community of San Francisco de
Asís, Ranchos de Taos . . . the Enduring Christ.

WHM

Contents

Introduction

Faces of Jesus

If you contemplate God with eyes of faith, you'll see Him just as He is, and, in a certain manner, face-to-face.   (Jean Eudes)

Once upon a time a man came to a rabbi with this question: "Rabbi, it is written that once we could see the face of God. Why can't we do that anymore? What happened to us that we can no longer reach that high to see the face of God?"

The rabbi was very old. He had seen so much in his life. He closed his eyes, running his hand through his white beard and sighed heavily. "My son, that is not the way it is at all. You cannot see the face of God because there are so few who can stoop that low. How sad this is, but it is the truth. Learn to bend, to bow, to kneel and stoop and you will be able to see God face-to-face!"

This book is about images of Jesus, or, more to the point, it is about seeing God face-to-face. Icons, images of Jesus, are part of the earliest tradition of the Eastern churches. They are a concrete theology of vision, as concrete and as revelatory as the Word of the Scriptures. The very word "icon" comes from the Greek word that means image. It is a word that is common and familiar to us from the Scriptures, beginning with Genesis, when we hear the story of "being made in the image of God" (9:6). In this sense we were created to be images of the Holy, reflecting truth and beauty in our very faces, bodies, and presences. Paul exhorts his newly baptized

Christians as they are faltering in their belief in the resurrection that "just as we have borne the image of the man of dust; we will also bear the image of the man of heaven" (1 Cor. 15:49).

These two symbols of Word and image keep coming up again and again in Paul's teachings. He reminds the early Christians and us that each of us is a letter of recommendation:

> You yourselves are our letter, written on our hearts, to be known and read by all; and you show that you are a letter of Christ, prepared by us, written not with ink but with the Spirit of the living God, not on tablets of stone but on tablets of human hearts.   (2 Cor. 3:2–3, NRSV)

Paul is intent on impressing upon them their new vocation, their way of life and being in the world since their baptism. It is an awesome and unbelievably high calling and responsibility, but one that is full of grace and truth:

> Now the Lord is the Spirit, and where the Spirit of the Lord is, there is freedom. And all of us, with unveiled faces, seeing the glory of the Lord as though reflected in a mirror, are being transformed into the same image from one degree of glory to another; for this comes from the Lord, the Spirit.
>
>   (2 Cor. 3:17–18, NRSV)

Paul is trying to teach what must be experienced and known in order to be expressed. He describes "the light of the gospel of the glory of Christ, who is the image of God." We have the honor of preaching Jesus Christ as Lord, a gift from God "who said 'Let light shine out of darkness,' who has shone in our hearts to give the light of the knowledge of the glory of God in the face of Jesus Christ" (2 Cor. 4:6, NRSV).

This book of icons of Jesus Christ is about belief, about devotion, and about contemplation of God, as it has been known and practiced in the heritage of the Eastern churches. Icons are revelations and exaltations of Christ as the image (*eikon*) of God, statements of creed and confession that express visually these words of the Scripture:

> He is the image of the invisible God, the firstborn of all creation; for in him all things in heaven and on earth were created, things visible and invisible, whether thrones or dominions or rulers or powers — all things have been created through him and for him. He himself is before all things, and in him all things hold together. He is the head of the body, the church; he is the beginning, the firstborn from the dead, so that he might come to have first place in everything. For in him all the fullness of God was pleased to dwell, and through him God was pleased to reconcile to himself all things, whether on earth or in heaven, by making peace through the blood of his cross. (Col. 1:15–19, NRSV)

A Christian is called to become this image of God by putting on the new life of Christ, "in whom is hidden all the treasures of wisdom and knowledge" (Col. 2:3). Those who were baptized in Christ and were "raised with Christ [must] seek the things that are above, where Christ is, seated at the right hand of God,...for you have died, and your life is hidden with Christ in God. When Christ who is your life is revealed, then you also will be revealed with him in glory" (3:1–4). Those who belong to Christ are "clothed with the new self, which is being renewed in knowledge according to the image of its creator.... Christ is all in all" (3:10–11).

The early church sought to say this in many ways. Clement of Rome writes: "Through Christ we see as in a mirror the spotless and excellent face of God."[1] Then Athanasius wrote in more theological language:

The Almighty and Most High Word of the Father pervades the whole of reality, everywhere unfolding his power and shining on all things visible and invisible. He sustains it all and binds it together in himself. He leaves nothing devoid of his power but gives life and keeps it in being throughout all of creation and in each individual creature.

The church in the West concentrated on words — philosophy, theology, catechetics, creed, and doctrine. While the church in the East appreciated these verbal forms of description, explanation, and teaching, it also sought to express in image — in the icon — the mysteries of Christ's incarnation, life, death, resurrection, and enthronement in glory at the right hand of the Father. Hearing was crucial, but just as crucial was seeing the Word of God.

The work of imaging the Word of God was the Spirit's response in history and culture to contemplation of "the glory of God shining on the face of Christ" (2 Cor. 4:6). The Eastern churches sought to teach the truth of the gospel by expressing it in beauty that drew the eye and the heart of the worshiper and the believer into the power of the mysteries of the faith. The Orthodox Church was intent on keeping in paradoxical tension the interconnectedness of matter and spirit, of body and soul, of political and religious life, and of historical and liturgical time.

There was a bitter and bloody time of turmoil when the church sought to define with precision what it believed, and a battle surged around whether icons should be made and venerated. Two theologians who wrote in defense of imagining and painting images of Christ, Mary, and the saints were St. John of Damascus and St. Theodore of Studios in the seventh and eighth centuries. The crux of the division was about the reality and power of creation and incarnation. The creeds and councils of the church had continuously stated unequivocally that the Second Person of the Holy

Trinity had entered into the world of matter, taken on our human flesh and blood, and raised our humanity into the life of the God-head: "The Word made flesh has deified the flesh" (St. John of Damascus). John Baggley describes the conflict:

> The reality of the Incarnation was at stake.... They believed that those who attacked the icons were attacking the reality of the Incarnation and the possibility of that revelation being communicated through matter....
>
> The defenders of the icons were defending a view of revelation that worked through sight as well as sound, through the eye as well as the ear. Since God had been revealed in the flesh, matter and art as well as word were the means the Spirit used to continue the art of revelation. Theodore argued that both hearing and sight are essential for a full assimilation of what God has revealed in Christ.... [Theodore, quoting Basil the Great, says] "Whatever the words of the narrative offer, the picture silently shows by imitation."[2]

The controversy, which was decided in favor of those who honored and venerated the icons, is celebrated on the Sunday of the Triumph of Orthodoxy, the first Sunday of Lent in Eastern Christianity. The liturgical hymn the "Kontakion" sings out: "The indefinable word of the Father made Himself definable, having taken flesh of Thee, O Mother of God, and having refashioned the soiled image to its former estate, has suffused it with Divine Beauty." Since then, icons have spoken a language of theology and of creed, of liturgy, of devotion and mysticism throughout the ages.

The icon speaks and the believer reads it, just as the iconographer writes it on wood. But the language is not only theological; it is also the language of beauty, of art, and of delight in matter redeemed by God in the person of Jesus Christ. It seeks to evoke a response through loveliness and gracefulness. These images are not just pictures of babes in arms or of a human being named Jesus; these are holy representations of the Word of God made flesh, Emmanuel, God-with-us, the Son of the Most High God who looks straight at us from the icon. Whether we stand or bend before it, it has been written to make us yearn to be transformed into that shining image redeemed by the blood of Christ, to bring the kingdom of justice with peace, to shout Good News with our very presence in the world, to serve and obey God's will first and foremost. Before that gaze, nothing matters except to believe and to obey.

The icon draws believers into the presence of God, places them before the throne of the Holy, and confronts them face-to-face with the holiness, the otherness, and yet the humanity and the divinity of the Word made flesh, Jesus. It is an experience of encounter, of meeting, of being sought after and singled out, and it can be humbling, freeing, transforming, and a moment of sheer goodness and delight at being in this presence of Holiness, the essence of goodness itself. Thomas Aquinas reminds us that "although our view of the sublimest things is limited and weak, it is most pleasant to be able to catch but a glimpse of them." And Bonaventure says: "In God alone is there primordial and true delight, and in all our delights it is this delight that we are seeking." To stand before the icon, to stand in the presence of God and be seen, is both delight and dissolution.

The encounter is experienced primarily in the liturgy. Icons, especially those of Jesus, are foundational to and sourced in the liturgy of the Eucharist and of the seasons of the year that culminate in the Pasch, the feast of Easter. The icon is invitation that sets the stage. It speaks of the mysteries of the Word and sacrament and situates this celebration in the midst of the universal mystery of creation redeemed and the power of the Risen Christ in the world today who transforms all by his presence and prayer at the right hand of the Father in glory. The icon is a way for the friends of Christ to share in his mysteries, in the sacraments, and to come to know the Father as Jesus knew him while in the flesh. This life in Christ, begun in our baptisms because of the resurrection of Christ, must grow, mature, and develop here on earth in history, as the kingdom comes ever more in its fullness. The liturgy and the icon not only teach but touch the faithful intimately with the knowledge of God, drawing us to himself. This is grace and life in the Spirit of Truth.

Nicholas Cabasilas (born ca. 1322) writes of this:

> In this way we live in God. We remove our life from this visible world to that world which is not seen by exchanging not the place but the very life itself and the mode. It was not ourselves who were moved towards God, nor did we ascend to Him; but it was He who came and descended to us. . . . He it was who came to earth and retrieved His own image, and He came to the place where the sheep were straying. . . . He did not remove us from here, but He made us heavenly while yet remaining on earth and imparted to us the heavenly life without leading us up to heaven, but by bending heaven to us and bringing it down.[3]

The icon plays a powerful part in this life here on earth. It does indeed bend heaven toward us so that we might see the face of God more clearly and take courage and hope from its sight. "Hope always draws the soul from the beauty that is seen to what is beyond, always kindles the desire for the hidden through what is perceived," wrote Gregory of Nyssa. The icon is placed on a level with the Scriptures and the cross as a form of revelation and knowledge of God. It takes its place with them and the Eucharist as a presence of God.

These icons are faces of Jesus from the Scriptures and the life of Jesus, from his death and resurrection, images of Jesus that are unique to the Orthodox churches. They are always Christ in glory, steeped in stillness, reflection, and long traditions of what is beautiful, what is balanced and in harmony, what is whole and holy in the world. These images "hold the world together" in the sense of Paul's words to the Colossians: "him in whom all things hold together" (1:17). There is a structure to each figure and each face that builds a theology and asserts belief. Even the faces can seem strange, odd, or different than our perceptions in the West of what is art. They are a language unto themselves. The accentuation of features — the eyes, nose, forehead — does not try to express individuality but eternity in humanity's flesh, in God made man. The eyes always strike us with force. There is usually a full gaze, with eyes forward, that transfixes our sight. We are held and washed in light. It is baptism by sight.

Each of the icons speaks of and reveals a facet of who Jesus is and what he has done in creation, by the power of the Spirit, in incarnation, in life, in death and resurrection, and now as the Lord of history and of all creation. We begin with icons that surround the coming of Jesus as the Word of the Most High God in flesh, born of the virgin Mary into the world. Thus the opening icons are "Christ Emmanuel, Flowering Cross" (Advent); "St. John the Forerunner"; "The Nativity of Our Lord Jesus Christ"; "St. Joseph, Shadow of the Father"; "Cristo Emanuel Niño Perdido" (the "lost child" in the temple); and "Jesus Christ Morning Star" (a teenage Christ who will be the protector of all endangered youth). Then we move immediately into Jesus as the teacher of mercy, "Christ All Merciful," with the words of Matthew 11, inviting all to come to him. This figure is also called the Pantocrator, He Who Rules over Everything.

Next are the icons of suffering, death, and glory in the resurrection. The first is unusual for Catholics in the West. It is called "Christ the Holy Silence," the silence of the suffering servant of Isaiah. In this version, the figure is a male. It is followed by "Jesus Christ Extreme Humility," showing Christ in death, and "The Passion of Matthew Shepard," a contemporary writing of the passion of many who are killed by hate; here the image is of a human being whose body is painted in the style of "Extreme Humility." Then there is "Jesus Christ Holy Forgiveness," forgiveness being the gift that Jesus prayed for all as he was dying. The last two icons in this section are "The Crucified Lord," another version of the cross icon, and "The Risen Christ."

The next section contains icons of history and those that deal with contemporary experiences of Christ. The first is called "The Mandylion (The Face Not Made by Human Hands)," whose legend says that Jude the Apostle brought this icon to heal someone who could not get to Jesus. Next is "Santo Mártir Rutilio Grande, S.J., con el Santo Niño de El Salvador," with Christ as a wounded child Savior. "Hagia Hesychia: Jesus Christ Redeemer Holy Silence," this time as the feminine Holy Wisdom, speaks of meditation and prayer. "Nuestro Salvador de las Sandias," a Risen Savior icon, is specific to the geography of New Mexico, where the iconographer and the writer both live. The next icon, the "Jesus Christ Seraphic Guardian of the Blood," has a varied history; from the times of Francis of Assisi, the Seraph brought the stigmata and its connection to many experiences of crucifixion worldwide in the two thousand years since Jesus' death.

And there are icons that at first glance appear to be more concerned with imaging persons other than Jesus Christ. These are "Mother of God, Soothe My Sorrows," "Sainte Thérèse de l'Enfant-Jésus et la Sainte-Face," and "Holy New Martyr Sister Mary Antoinette, Daughter of Wisdom." In the Orthodox tradition, each icon presented here is ultimately a doorway into the holy presence of God. These three icons — of Mary, Thérèse (known as the Little Flower), and Mary Antoinette, a more unfamiliar saint, a contemporary martyr from the Congo — are written and contemplated in their relationship with God. Mary is shown, of course, with her child, but it is the child of the nations, the child of history, and the child that brings a new age of radiant light into the world. Thérèse, the nineteenth-century Carmelite nun, is seen bearing the icon of the formal names she took during her vow ceremony. She lived and suffered and prayed to Christ as the Divine Child and the Holy Face of God, and it was this expression of the Word made flesh that taught her and made her a saint. Mary Antoinette was a member of the community of the Daughters of the Divine Wisdom. The community is dedicated to imitating and preaching the wisdom of God and so lives under the tutelage of the Spirit's blessing and knowledge. These three icons remind us that each of us is called to be an icon of God, living ultimately in relation to our God, singularly seeking with our lives to reveal one understanding of the mystery of the infinite and holy triune God — the Father, the Son, and the Spirit.

Each of the icons employs color and form, depicting clothing and posture, as well as a symbolic background — such as diamond shapes, oval mandorlas, rays of light, and halos and circles that center the face or figure. The sources of Scripture and tradition in the liturgy and in history are provided along with prayers and reflections on how each icon seeks to transform us, how each points to the shining image of the new creation, the new man and woman of grace and life, now in our time and place.

It must be remembered that these pictures tell stories, state a theology, write of a devotion, and provide a history of encountering God. They are creeds in paint and storytelling that teach as do the stained glass windows of cathedrals or the once-painted stone crosses of the Celts or the illuminated manuscripts of the age of learning. They are a reassurance, a presence, a proclamation, as in the Word proclaimed aloud: God is — God is here. And the tradition is that we surrender to an icon, dwell with it, as a mother bird sits on her nest waiting for her hatchlings to emerge. God broods over us in the icons. And so we are summoned to look at them every day for they bring life, food, and grace into our bodies. There is a shining forth in our flesh that emerges with undivided attention and devotion. We come to drink in the icon and to be taken and held by it. We stand before the eye of God, or sit, or kneel, and we bow and kiss the icon, touching our fingers to our forehead, lips, shoulders, and heart as we greet and acknowledge that we are there — before All That Is, before God, the Holy One. Always the icon seeks to bring us to prayer and attentive adoration. In her book *Waiting for God*, Simone Weil writes: "Prayer consists of attention. It is the orientation of all the attention of which the soul is capable toward God. The quality of the attention counts for much in the quality of the prayer. Warmth of heart cannot make up for it."[4] In this insight, Weil echoes the belief and the practice of those who pray with icons.

The icon looks at us with divine dedication, with radiance, with blessing and judgment. We are called to stay and not look away. How do we look at Truth itself, or Hope, or Mercy, or Justice? And then let Hope or Truth or Justice and Mercy look back at us, beholding us with contemplation that is fierce, serene, and faithful? We who are finite mortal beings are looked at by the Infinite; we are scrutinized with concern and compassion that seek to save us again and yet again.

The icon is always about glory, glory glimpsed here and the fullness of glory that will come. Symeon the New Theologian writes:

> God can be known to us in the same way as a man can see an endless ocean by standing at the shore at night with a dimly lit candle. Do you think he can see much? Not much, almost nothing. And nevertheless, he sees the water well. He knows that there is an ocean in front of him, that this ocean is huge

and that he cannot see it all at once. The same is true of our knowledge of God.[5]

To stand before these icons, these portraits of Jesus the Holy One of God, is to stand at that ocean's edge and to begin to walk into the waves, slowly, deliberately, knowing that to do so is to be transformed into light and freedom, as surely as hearing the Word of God and taking it to heart.

Nearly a decade ago Michel Quenot wrote:

> The icon is in vogue today.... Today, when the human countenance is so disfigured, when racial discrimination persists, when so many people suffer from a lack of genuine, sincere communication, faces on the icons radiating a light that comes from beyond fascinate and beckon us to contemplate. Although they speak indeed of God, they also speak about humanity.[6]

The faces of the icon, the images of Jesus the Word made flesh, expose us, lay bare our inhumanity to one another, and convict us of betraying our faith in the incarnation and the resurrection. So some of the faces are very hard to look at — we turn away, not wanting to see what we do, what we become when we refuse the image of God impressed upon us in baptism, confirmation, and Eucharist. They question us relentlessly: Do we really believe that the flesh of God has made holy the flesh of all human beings? Do we live with reverence toward one another, remembering that our God takes personally what we do to the flesh of our brothers and sisters as if it were done to his own flesh and blood? Do we bow before one another, as servants, in awe of the power of God in his creation, treating each and all with respect, dignity, and tenderness, as our God has done in the mystery of the incarnation, becoming our flesh and dwelling still among us? Do we truly believe that we were created to love and are to absorb that Love made visible in the person of Jesus into our own flesh, and turn and love one another with that Love, as gratitude given back? The face, the Word of Jesus, asks and waits upon us for response in prayer and in life.

The title of this book is *Christ All Merciful,* and the underlying theme that permeates each of these icons is mercy. It is the mercy that is God in the person of Jesus Christ crucified and risen, Savior of all. It is the mercy of God the Father who sent his beloved into the world and raised Jesus from the dead, and the mercy that is the Holy Spirit of God who comforts, heals, forgives, and tenders those who suffer, serve, and obey God, and seek to bring the kingdom of justice with mercy upon the face of the earth. We will reflect on as many aspects of mercy as there are icons to gaze at and so be drawn into the grasp, the embrace, the clasp, and the breath and touch of Mercy.

There is an ancient Zen story from Japan that can perhaps show us how an icon can affect us over a long period of time. Like many Zen stories it doesn't actually have a title. I call it the "Mirror of Truth":

Once upon a time there was a princess. She loved to travel and often was carried to distant parts of her father's kingdom in search of treasures of mind and artifacts of beauty. One day as she was being carried along a dusty hot road, she glanced outside the curtains and noticed an old woman huddled at the side of the road, bent double and ill. She saw and in a moment had pity on the woman. She had her lifted into her own litter and carried to the palace. She didn't know exactly why she did this — there were so many old and sickly beggars in the kingdom, but this one seemed to call to her with her eyes. She cared for her, nursing her to health and feeding her until her strength returned.

As the old woman set to leave, she approached the princess and drew from her clothes a gift for the princess, a mirror. It was simple, wooden, with a carved design along its edges, but well-worn, and used. She offered it in gratitude for her care and ministrations. It was all she had. The princess was embarrassed — she had so many mirrors! But she accepted it graciously and the old woman disappeared. The princess laid the mirror down without a second thought.

Later that night she began to prepare for a royal dinner and reception. She dressed in finery, as befitting her rank, and waited so that she would enter just as all the other guests were seated. She slipped out of her chambers and realized she hadn't looked to see if all was in order. She ran back in and, without thinking, picked up the mirror she had cast on a table, the mirror that the old woman had given her. She stopped in her tracks.

She couldn't stop looking at what she saw. It was a beautiful sight, color, designs — but it was a peacock! Not a woman. She was tempted to throw the mirror aside, but hesitated and looked again. It was a peacock and in that moment the truth seared her. She was just a peacock strutting her beauty and raiment before the people. Chastened, she went to the party, but she vowed that night to change her life, to alter what she had become as drastically and truthfully as she knew how.

Soon she was pleading with her father to let her leave the palace and join a monastery of nuns, to study, to sit, to reflect, and to serve those who were poor and in need of compassion. Her father was reluctant but she was persistent. In time she left the kingdom and disappeared into the monastery. Years passed. She studied, read, sat *zazen*, served in the kitchen and the garden, tending to the needs of visitors, begging for her food. Because she was once a princess and knew languages and how to read and so many other skills, she began to rise through the ranks. Within seven years she had become the abbess of a large monastery.

One evening before bed she was standing in the doorway and a great sadness came over her. What was it? She remembered the mirror, the gift of the old woman, and wondered where she was now; if she was still alive. And she turned into her small cell and went through her few possessions to find the mirror. She took a deep breath and looked into it. Again she was stunned. It was beautiful. This time she saw an eagle, wings spread, elegant and proud, flying high above all the other birds, above the earth itself, soaring alone in its own world. She was broken-hearted. All these years and still she was more a bird than a human being.

Again, she sought to change her life, to live in such a way that she would be whole, truthful, and compassionate. With time, she moved out of the great monastery and, instead of being an abbess, she became a wandering monk, a hermit who played with the children, who shared her small portion of vegetables or grain with passersby and lived simply in the mountains, sitting, emptying out.

The years passed, and one day as she was out looking for food and caring for an old man down in the valley, there was a forest fire. By the time she returned to her small hut, there was nothing left but ashes, still smoking. She had nothing but the robe she wore. She stood in the ashes with the wind blowing around her and, looking down, noticed a flash of light. She bent down and there was the mirror, the wood charred, but the glass intact. She hesitated. Did she want to know what she had become, if she had changed at all? Slowly she lifted the mirror to her face and gazed into it. She smiled. It was beautiful. What was there clear and true was a wild iris, singular, ordinary, blooming, waving in the wind. And in that moment her feet stood solidly on the ground and she sensed her roots go deep into the earth, down and down, through the core of the planet and then spiraling out into the universe and all was one. She was a wild iris, a woman, a human being, and she was at home. She was nothing, nothing at all.

The icon is a mirror held before our eyes so that we can see our faces, our souls, and our lives as God sees us. The experience is always truthful, faithful, and clear. The icon is a gift, the face of God, the eye of God looking back at us in compassion and clarity, demanding that we become what God dreamed us to be when we were created in the image of God. The icon stays with us until we are whole, until we are one, until we are home. God is watching us. God is looking at us. God is All in All.

Let us pray, in the words of the psalms, the old and venerable prayers of those who have gone before us in faith, struggling and seeking the face of God, as we do:

O God, you are my God, I seek you, my soul thirsts for you;
my flesh faints for you, as in a dry and weary land
where there is no water.
So I have looked upon you in the sanctuary,
beholding your power and glory.
Because your steadfast love is better than life,
my lips will praise you.
So I will bless you as long as I live;
I will lift up my hands and call on your name.   (Ps. 63, NRSV)[7]

1

Christ Emmanuel, Flowering Cross

This icon is first because icons speak along a time axis. The beginning of the church year is Advent, the season of expectation for the coming of Christ. The readings cry out that we be alert: Be on guard! Be attentive! For one day at the fulfillment of time itself the Son of Man will come in glory to judge the nations with his very presence in the world, and time as we mark it will end. As the season progresses we are summoned to turn our lives and spirits toward repentance so that we can perceive the coming of Christ more than two thousand years ago into the history of earth and creation, a coming realized in the mystery of the incarnation, the child born of the Virgin Mary. And throughout all the seasons of the church calendar we are reminded that Christ comes in the Word, the Scriptures of Good News to the poor, and in sacrament, especially in the bread of Eucharist and the wine of Communion.

This flowering cross is one side of a processional cross — the other depicting the Crucified Lord. Such a cross is used to lead the community into the church and precedes the people as they process toward the sanctuary to celebrate the holy mysteries. In this sense it is a moveable feast drawing us backward and forward in time, into a time of grace and truth, a time of transformation and becoming more whole and holy, together. History and mystery combine and are experienced together in liturgy. This icon initiates the work of liturgy and paradoxically draws our attention to the promises and echoes of the past and the open-endedness of what the future

can be fashioned into because of the redeeming and ever-lasting presence of Christ Emmanuel, Child, crucified and risen to life that never ends, claiming all creation and all peoples in its grasp.

Emmanuel is the ancient word meaning "God-Is-with-Us." It is a statement of fact and a declaration of belief: God yesterday, today, and tomorrow, binding time together. It is the clarion call, a name cried out in hope that was the proclamation of the prophet Isaiah to a king, Ahaz. It was a sign that was given, though the king refused the sign. Ahaz, king in Israel, had been in the throes of negotiation with other countries, seeking a political advantage for his small country, which had very little clout. He was jockeying for a position that would enable them to survive, though they would have to tithe and bend before Samaria. Ahaz had already decided what he would do, ignoring the prophet's exhortation to rely on Yahweh alone and not get entangled with the other nations, an entanglement that would cause Israel's destruction. But Isaiah the prophet and God would not be so easily dismissed. The promise was given, the hope expressed, and the seed planted for the immediate future of one who would obey the Word of God in the name of the people and in the far future for one who would literally be the justice and truth of God in flesh and blood, a child among humankind, Emmanuel, God-Is-with-Us.

God's patience is often tried by his people, as in this case with Ahaz, but God is patient and there will be one who "rejects evil and cherishes virtue." And this child will be the one who binds Yahweh with the people in unbreakable bonds of liberation and love. This is the child set in the center-piece, the heart of the cross. This is the Christ who has always existed and the incarnated Christ who has become flesh and the Christ who is the saving presence of God among us for all time. His head is surrounded by a trinity of crosses revealing God invisible and visible, hidden and revealed. He is a child, but a mature, focused, and aware child, poised at the center of history, altering all time and space irrevocably in his person.

Most remarkable, perhaps, in the positioning of the child are the arms extending outward grasping the stalks and the intertwining bush of leaves and berries, bright red drops and vibrant life reaching to every corner of the cross. This cross flowers with hope, with joy, with glory and exultation and fruitfulness. This is the green and red of Advent's fruit — the birth of a child in blood and flesh who will live and grow and wrap a world with truth and compassion, and die, shedding his blood and giving his flesh for the life of a world to come that enters this world in his coming among us. This is the long-awaited fulfillment of prophecy. This is the one to be worshiped by the remnant that lives on the hope of God's intervention in the world, who stake their lives on the faithfulness of God, and who are stunned by the actual fulfillment of the prophecies in a child that is both human and divine, one born of flesh and of God, of the Father and the Spirit. This is the child of the "O" Antiphons that are sung at vespers throughout the universal church for the days preceding Christmas, December 17 to 23. They are sung simply, antiphonally interspersed among the lines of the Magnificat as the day disappears into the dark, hushed yet flushed with surety. These are the names and the meanings of this child:

O Wisdom, uttered by the mouth of the Most High, and reaching to the ends of the earth, come and teach us the way of prudence.

O Adonai, ruler of the house of Israel, who appeared to Moses in the burning bush, come and redeem us.

O Root of Jesse, standard of the Nations and of kings, whom the whole world implores, come and deliver us.

O Key of David and Sceptre of the house of Israel, what you open none can shut, come and lead us out of darkness.

O Radiant Dawn, splendor of eternal light and Sun of justice, shine on those lost in darkness, come to enlighten us.

O King of the nations, so long desired, cornerstone uniting humankind, come and save the work of your creation.

O Emmanuel, God present in our midst, long awaited Savior and King, come and save us, O Lord our God.[8]

This is the ancient child, the child with the long reach of hope, the hand held out with light, summoning the universe and all that has been made to look back in wonder at the eyes of the Holy One steadily beholding us. This is God questioning us: Do you know who I am? I am the glory and the judge of the nations, the Holy One of God, the hope of the ages. And do you know who you are? This is a declaration that there is reciprocity in the entirety of the universe. All is held together in the blood that binds a family, in the joy that is birthed with a Christ-mass child who dies gloriously, drenching the wood of cradle and cross in the blood of God given as the wine of delight among all who desire the reign of this One — this One who is given to love us into a life that can only be sung and lived with all of creation before the holiness of God.

All of life and death, of history and eternity, lies in the eyes of this Child, Emmanuel praying that we flower and bear fruit and become one. The vines, the stalks, the limbs of this flowering tree are the arms and the trunk of this Child's body, the veins and arteries that contain all of creation. This is a cross that calls us to sing, to enter into the mysteries of the year, and to walk through history, mindful that now and always our God is with us:

So when next he comes with glory,
And the world is wrapped in fear,
May he with his mercy shield us,
And with words of love draw near.

Honor, glory, might, and blessing
To the Father and the Son,
With the everlasting Spirit
While unending ages run. Amen.[9]

2

St. John
the Forerunner

We want to bathe in the blood of the dragon and drink from
the blood of the Lamb at the same time. But the truth is that
we have to choose.   (Dorothee Sölle)

This is John the Baptizer, given the title "Prodromos," meaning
Forerunner, literally translated "in advance," the one crying in the
wilderness. This wilderness is the desert, the roots of Israel's genesis
as a people belonging solely to Yahweh, wedded in covenant to God
as a sign to the nations. The lineage of Israel begins in their being
drawn forth from the waters of the Reed Sea into the wilderness
of the Sinai Desert, where they were courted by the one God. The
rocky mountains of their sojourn were the place where Yahweh
visibly dwelled among them, as a cloud by day and fire by night.
After Moses, the prophet of the wilderness was Elijah, fed by ravens,
hiding out in a wadi, the "troubler of Israel" calling the nation again
and again to faithfulness, integrity, and reliance on God alone. In
Israel's spirituality, the desert is the privileged place and time of
revelation and intimacy with the Holy, a place where its roots as
a people that would be a light to the nations are firmly and solidly
established, in rock and wasteland, so that it will be able to endure
anywhere.

And then, the last in the tradition of prophets, John the relative of Jesus comes also from the desert. His birth is heralded by the angel Gabriel to his father Zechariah:

> Your wife, Elizabeth, will bear a son and you shall name him John. He will bring joy and gladness to you and many will rejoice at his birth.
>
> This son of yours will be great in the eyes of the Lord. Listen: he shall never drink wine or strong drink, but he shall be filled with holy spirit even from his mother's womb. Through him many of the people of Israel will turn to the Lord their God. He himself will open the way to the Lord with the spirit and power of the prophet Elijah; he will reconcile fathers and children, and lead the disobedient to wisdom and righteousness, in order to make ready for the Lord a people prepared.
>
> (Luke 1:13b–17)

This prophet straddles the bridge between the earlier and the newer testaments, the revelation and the covenants of the Word of God. He comes with immediacy, with shocking urgency, bringing moral and ethical imperatives for the people. They must turn their hearts back to the Holy One! They must "give some evidence that they mean to reform" (Matt. 3:8)!

John's appearance in the Jordan is described like the coming of a tsunami, a ferocious wave coming upon the shore and engulfing all in its wake. John is the shock of Advent, a shock to everyone's system — individuals, kings and nations, corporate structures, all of creation itself. John, the forerunner, preaches, exhorts, reprimands, cries out, attacks with the word of his mouth as though he is shouting to those who are long dead and who are dominated by other allegiances than the one they owe to God alone.

This John is a faster, one who does penance and survives almost on sheer spirit and force of will in the desert. From the beginning he has heard the Word of God echoing in his bones and flesh, rising in his mind, and so it flows from his lips. Barefoot, bony, bearded, and clothed in animal skins, he is worn down to bone and raw survival and existence. He came proclaiming a baptism of repentance for the forgiveness of sins. His work is washing out the eyes and hearts of a people who have forgotten to live on the Word of God, who have become slaves once again and worship other gods in collusion with Rome and Herod, who has betrayed faith. And John's commands are very specific as to both group affiliation and what needs to be done now if anyone is going to be able to see the One coming after him. He is interested in getting back to the basics. It begins, this new season, with sharing: shared bread, shared clothing and shelter. There is to be no greed, no lies, and no violence in the land (Luke 3:10–14). And when he first lays eyes on the One, he cries out: "There is the Lamb of God, who takes away the sin of the world" (John 1:29).

John's gaze is intense, focused on the interior, on what we must strain to be able to see, but can know even more surely than John himself when we repent and hear the Word of God in Jesus the Christ. John's body has wings. He is an angel, messenger of God, the angel of the wilderness and turning. He is gaunt, with ragged hair and uncut beard, standing on rock, alongside the waters of baptism, where he will meet Jesus. This winged person is a force to be reckoned with in his own right, but he stands at the edge, the edge of the old and the edge of the unknown, facing the Spirit of God. He seeks to turn the faces of the people toward the radiant coming of the dawn of the Son of Justice and to set their feet on the way of the kingdom of God. John has no other life but pointing to another. There are words in a poem by Juan Ramón Jiménez that describe him perhaps better than most:

My feet, so deep in the earth.
My wings so high in the heavens
And so much pain
In the heart torn between.[10]

This is John, the prophet and ascetic, called from the womb of his mother to dance in the presence of another child in the womb of Mary. He heard the One he was to live for in the voice of greeting: "Shalom, peace be with you!" And forever after his voice would serve only the truth and the Word of God made flesh. The description of John grown to be a man, the forerunner in Luke, sings and dances like lightning and thunder in summer storms:

And you, my child,
shall be called prophet of the Most High,
for you shall go before the Lord
to prepare the way for him
and enable his people to know of their salvation
when he comes to forgive their sins.
This is the work of the mercy of our God,
who comes from on high as a rising sun
shining on those who live in darkness
and in the shadow of death,
and guiding our feet into the way of peace.

(Luke 1:76–79)

John is the "work of the mercy of God." And John's understanding of himself is pure and simple and evocative: "My joy is full now, He must increase and I must decrease" (John 3:30). John is the lightning trail of truth that leads to the doorway of the kingdom of God, opening into the presence of Jesus, the justice of God that radiates in a human face and cloaks the whole world with truth. He will die in prison, in the darkness, but he will know that the Light is loose in the world and his life's meaning is finished being sung. And we are reminded that the least in the kingdom is "greater than John"!

(This icon is a copy of the extraordinary fifteenth-century icon of the Baptist with wings as the "Angelic Man," a human existing almost totally on spirit. The water and the Holy Spirit were added to the original because this was a commission from the Franciscan Friars in Medjugorje, Bosnia. It was to commemorate what was believed to be the first appearance of the Mother of God ushering in the New Advent, an appearance that occurred on the feast of the Nativity of John the Baptist, June 24, 1981.)

3

The Nativity of Our Lord Jesus Christ

The light shines in the darkness,
and the darkness has not overcome it.

(John 1:5)

This is the birth of a human child, but this is also the birth of the Second Person of the Trinity, the Holy One of God. The mystery of the incarnation, of God clothed in the flesh and blood of humankind, and the coming of Light to a darkened world are all present in this overarching cave beneath a starry sky. In the Eastern church this icon is sometimes called "The Paradise That Is within the Cave," and the liturgical texts strongly emphasize the Christ's divinity. This is no ordinary child; this is the Sun of Righteousness and Justice "who will shine upon you who respect my Name and bring health in its rays" (Mal. 4:2). And yet, paradoxically, the iconographer uses these words to describe the feel of this mystery that he sought to write:

A cave singed by the fire of the Gloria,
A hovering star on this night of nights,
A most tender silent couple in adoration of the newborn King.[11]

This is a place where we are invited to witness an event of magnitude beyond telling. This is a place where we are stilled and quieted in the presence of the babe:

> For a child is born to us,
>
> a son is given us;
>
> the royal ornament is laid upon his shoulder,
>
> and his name is proclaimed:
>
> "Wonderful Counselor, Mighty God,
>
> Everlasting Father, Prince of Peace." (Isa. 9:5)

These words sound forth at midnight Mass, and they sound as they once did in the mouths of prophets, angels, and people near delirious with joy, seeking to find words that could adequately describe what words cannot depict. The Eastern church solemnly declares this icon "The Nativity according to the Flesh of Our Lord and God and Savior Jesus Christ, 25 December." This is a birth for the people, the "people who have walked in darkness" who have now "seen a great light. A light has dawned on those who live in the land of the shadow of death" (Isa. 9:1). This is the night of liberation and freedom. This is the night of a harvest of hope and justice. This is the night of rejoicing and casting off sorrow and the yoke of slavery. This is the night when peace reigns and all the world gathers and is drawn to this cave and this couple kneeling at this child's bed, in a manger, a feeding trough, the child cradled in straw and wrapped in swaddling cloths. This is, in the words of the prophet Isaiah, what "the zealous love of Yahweh Sabaoth will do" for the people of the earth (Isa. 9:8).

The three figures form a trinity of wonder. Joseph kneels, bent both over the child who is the Light of the world and over a single candle flame, sheltered with his hand from the drafts and wind of the night. This is the man who will provide shelter for this infant until he grows to be physically what he already is: the flesh of the Son of God, Redeemer and Liberator, born of woman, who will share the destiny of all humankind — fullness of life and death.

The manger is made of the same wood as the instrument of torture and death, the cross, and he is wrapped in cloths that will one day be his death shroud. He is food, placed carefully in a feeding trough for lambs and sheep. He is a man-child, the fulfillment of the prophecies born this night. In this moment the child is father to the man, Joseph, as surely as Joseph will be a fathering presence in this man's life on earth.

The woman kneels with outstretched open hands that hover over the body of the child as though she already knows this is not only her child. This child belongs to the world, to all the nations and people who have waited for centuries for the light that would shatter the darkness of hatred, evil, war, and death itself. This is the virgin, the young woman who has given birth and now worships her child who is her maker and whom she will learn to follow to the cross and resurrection as a believer. This child is mother to the maiden as surely as she has given birth to him and will mother him in his human weakness and need, for he, the Word, will bring forth love in her beyond all telling and be her life beyond the limitations of flesh and blood.

This child-God will share all our sufferings and joys, our days and nights, our possibilities of grace, and our death. This cave and manger laid with the child's body are altar, table, tomb, and throne. This is the Word of God made flesh and dwelling among us (John 1), the God that cannot be contained made poor and lowly in love for us, the God who has come among us as brother and master of the universe, and the God now humbly made the servant of the servants, as the tender mercy of God Most High. And yet hidden inside this momentous event is something else to make us pause:

The heavens open and what is disclosed? A baby, God manifest in the flesh. The stable, the manger, the straw; poverty, cold, darkness — these form the setting of the divine gift.

In this child, God gives his supreme message to the soul — Spirit to spirit — but in a human way. Outside in the fields the heavens open and the shepherds look up astonished to find the music and radiance of reality all around them. But inside, our closest contact with that same reality is being offered to us in the very simplest, homeliest way — emerging right into our ordinary life. A baby — just that.[12]

There is the star marking time's turning, marking the place as the royal doors of the king's entrance. The magi of the East, those who sought wisdom in the night sky, will follow that star to the burning Light hidden in the earth and recognize the wisdom of God shining in the eyes of a child who is both human and divine. The star serves the purpose of an angel, and of a dream announcing the message of salvation for all who have the eyes to see and who have been searching for God. Absolutely everything in the icon is bent toward and seen in relation to the child who looks straight out at us who come to see, to believe, to worship and kneel before, as do Mary and Joseph, his parents on earth.

But the Orthodox Church looks upon this scene and layers in an entire history of God's coming to earth looking for a people that belongs to God alone. That church chants and prays:

Bethlehem has opened Eden: come, and let us see. We have found joy in secret: come, and let us take possession of the paradise that is within the cave. There the unwatered Root has appeared, from which forgiveness flowers forth: there is found the undug Well, whence David longed to drink of old (1 Sam. 23:15). There the Virgin has borne a Babe, and made the thirst of Adam and David to cease straightway. Therefore let us hasten to this place where now is born a young Child, the pre-eternal God.[13]

In this icon, birth and death meet; the altar of sacrifice and the table of feasting are one, and the Lamb of God comes to save us from our night of darkness and death. This is a cave, womb, tomb, grave, and place where God and humankind once again meet in love. This is the *kenosis*, the self-emptying of God, humbling himself to come among us, and accepting even death on the cross, buried deep in mystery. Yet the star attests to the glory that will one day erupt in resurrection and life that knows no death. Heaven and earth come close together and justice and mercy are flesh and blood among us. From of old, the church has sought to put into words the Word born this night:

> Of the Father's love begotten,
> Ere the worlds began to be,
> He is Alpha and Omega,
> He the source, the ending he.
> Of the things that are,
> That have been,
> And that future years shall see.
>
> Christ, to thee with God the Father,
> And O holy Ghost, to thee,
> Hymn and chant and high thanksgiving,
> And unwearied praises be:
> Honor, glory, and dominion
> And eternal victory. Amen.[14]

Come, let us adore him. Come, let us kneel before him. Come, let us be silent before our God like stars of night. Let us reach for him in wonder, and bend and shelter this Light given unto us in incarnation and in baptism, to keep until the flame grows strong and rises through the dark eternally.

4

St. Joseph, Shadow of the Father

We have found the one that Moses wrote about in the Law, and the prophets as well; he is Jesus, son of Joseph, from Nazareth. (John 1:45)

We know so little of Joseph, the just, the dreamer, and the protector of Mary and her child. Yet he is father to the Son of God, the model and teacher of Jesus the Jew, the long-awaited prophet and Son of Justice. Joseph, of course, is named in the tradition for another Joseph: the son of the patriarch in the Book of Genesis who dreams of glory, of being lord over his brothers, and of his parents bowing before him (Gen. 37:5–11). The earlier Joseph's father, we are told, was disturbed, but "pondered the matter in his heart." This Joseph is sold into slavery by his brothers, yet rises to the heights in the house of Pharaoh in Egypt, and we are told repeatedly that "God was with him" at all times (Gen. 39:3, 21). This Joseph listens to his dreams, obeys the Word of the Lord that he hears in them, and prospers even in the land of his affliction. He forgives his brothers their attempt to kill him and feeds them bread in their hunger. He tells them, wondrously:

God has sent me ahead of you to make our race survive there and to save many of you. So it was not you but God who sent

me here, and made me a father to Pharaoh and Lord of his household, and ruler also of all the land of Egypt. (Gen. 45:7–8)

This is Joseph's namesake in the history of his people, Israel. And Joseph, father of Jesus, is born of a long line of dreamers, once kings, but now living in occupied territory, under the harsh heel of Rome. But he still lives on dreams, God's dreams for a chosen people that belongs to a God of promises who is always faithful; God had promised them a land and one who would be the Sun of Justice, the presence of God with the people so clearly that all the nations would come to learn of this wisdom and peace. Joseph is Jewish and he lives on the psalms, the words and stories of the prophets, Isaiah, Jeremiah, Micah, and the others. He is one of the remnant, the faithful ones who staked their lives on these dreams and lived from Sabbath to Sabbath, hoping against hope that the Messiah would come in their lifetime.

This was a people that believed that dreams were a forgotten language of God, a way of giving absolutely essential information to a person so that he or she could do what was necessary for the group's survival. Once the dream was given, the people staked their lives on it and obeyed, though they would be hard-pressed to explain their reasoning to others. In the tradition of Israel, dreams, stars, and angels were all the same — messages from God reveal-ing God's presence and will, here and now, intruding into history, disclosing a hidden meaning for all. We know from the Scriptures that Joseph is born of the house of David. This is the title that the angel addresses him by in his dream: son of David. He is a carpen-ter, poor, a laborer who lives day to day, struggling to survive. And, most probably, he is young, like Mary, at most fourteen or fifteen, betrothed after he had come of age in the Jewish community at twelve.

In the gospel of Matthew we learn of him, but only in relation to how "the birth of Jesus the Messiah took place":

> When his mother, Mary, had been engaged to Joseph, but before they lived together, she was found to be with child from the Holy Spirit. Her husband, Joseph, being a righteous man and unwilling to expose her to public disgrace, planned to dismiss her quietly. But just when he had resolved to do this, an angel of the Lord appeared to him in a dream and said, "Joseph, son of David, do not be afraid to take Mary as your wife, for the child conceived in her is from the Holy Spirit. She will bear a son, and you are to name him Jesus, for he will save his people from their sins." All this took place to fulfill what had been spoken by the Lord through the prophet:
>
> > "Look, the virgin shall conceive and bear a son,
> > and they shall name him Emmanuel,"
>
> which means, "God is with us." When Joseph awoke from sleep, he did as the angel of the Lord commanded him; he took her as his wife.   (Matt. 1:18–24, NRSV)

This is the longest text we have on Joseph, and it is layered with insight and meaning. Joseph finds himself caught in a terrible quandary. He is engaged but has not yet celebrated marriage with Mary. This engagement period could last for months, or years, but Mary's situation was serious enough that it merited a divorce to sever the relationship. The law was specific in regard to a woman found to be pregnant before the marriage ritual. She was to be stoned to death along with the unborn child. It is not known just how often this was actually carried out, but it was ominous. Other translations say that Joseph did not want to expose her to the law and decided to put her away quietly, which would have meant

rejection from the community, a life of servitude, slavery, or pros-
titution. In any case, she would have had to make it on her own
with the child.

But we are also told that Joseph is a righteous or a just man, and
so he agonizes over obedience to the law, knowing the hardship
and the horror that can occur with mindless acceptance of the
law. Joseph is one of those who waits for the fullness of time and
the coming of the One who will be Justice itself in human form.
Joseph "eats, sleeps, and drinks" the tradition of his faith. He makes
his decision and goes to sleep. And he dreams in that faith. Even
the angel quotes Scripture to help him decide upon an alternative
course of action.

Joseph's story is marvelous! It is a stunning break in "how things
are." He awakes to obey the command of God, to break the law to
save this woman and her child who is conceived by the power of
the Spirit. He goes to sleep facing two terrible options and awakes
to something freeing, liberating, and filled with life for all involved.
He adopts this child of God as his own and takes them both in to
shelter them and raise the child with Mary, the child's mother.

This is Joseph's first dream. He has two more, the first when
he is warned to arise immediately in the middle of the night and
flee with the child and his mother into the land of Egypt to save
their lives from Herod, who is raging and disturbed at the very
possibility that someone would be born king and be a future threat
to his power (Matt. 2:13). And again we are told that after they
spent long years as exiles, refugees in Egypt, the angel comes again
to tell them it is safe to return home to Israel. Then Joseph learns
in another dream that Herod's son is now king and so decides
to settle in Nazareth to protect the child (Matt. 2:19). These are
pragmatic dreams, always about saving lives and living in safety so
that the child can mature and grow. Joseph was a day-laborer and

taught his son his trade as a carpenter, with Jesus working with him as soon as he was able. It would have been hard labor, six days a week building a city, and they would have lived for their one day, the Sabbath of the Lord.

This is the Joseph who raised Jesus in the tradition of Israel, taught him to be a Jew, to pray, to make ethical choices, and to wrap his entire life around the Word of the Lord revealed in the prophets and psalms. Jesus learned from him the stories and laws, and how to interpret them for life. He would have learned the most from observing this man keep the Sabbath holy, pray, sing the goodness of God, and work sharing the fruits of his labors with the poor in their community. And this would be learned in a land of injustice, servitude, and harsh occupation by Roman soldiers. We are told on a number of occasions that Jesus "was subject to them" (Luke 2:51). This is the man who raised Jesus to be the righteous shoot of the house of Jacob (Isa. 27:6).

This is Joseph the refugee, the illegal alien in Egypt, the one flee-ing for his life and seeking to protect his family from the violence of nationalistic hatred and insanity, the sojourner in a foreign land who settled in a town where no one would think to look for anyone of import. They were asylum-seekers, struggling with another lan-guage, living a hand-to-mouth existence, despised, spending much of the first decade of their lives together away from relatives in an enclave of Jews. They fled from terror and lived in its shadow all their lives. This man took on the task of raising the child of God and so took on the task of God's dreams for the people. He, as much as Mary, staked his life on the Word of the Lord and obeyed the command of God, handing over his whole life to make sure that the child would grow to be a man and save his people from their sins.

The icon was "written" as a prayer of longing for the coming of the child with Joseph bringing peace to the world. It is an icon that is a trinity: the Father unseen except in faith, Joseph the shadow of the Father, and the child of God, fathered by this man who gave him a place and a relationship of peace. Jesus grew in this shadow of peace, grew strong and grew in wisdom. One wonders how often he was asked: "Are you Jesus, son of Joseph?"

And Joseph, how often did he pray, "Let the heavens send righteousness like dew and the clouds rain it down. Let the earth open and salvation blossom, so that justice also may sprout" (Isa. 45:8), as he watched this child grow into a man? We stand before them, clothed in brilliant reds as they challenge us to make of this world a place of peace where justice thrives and all children are safe, flourishing, and loved.

Joseph, Shadow of the Father, teach us as you taught Jesus, your beloved adopted son, to obey, to live on dreams, and to stake our lives on the promises of God. Amen.

5

Cristo Emanuel Niño Perdido

But he is Christ, the power of God and the wisdom of God.

(1 Cor. 1:24)

This is the Christ Child who has profound ageless wisdom, mature holiness, and the infinite compassion of the adult Christ. This, too, is the "lost boy" who in Luke instructed the elders in the temple, teaching in the role of his Father's wisdom. The story is familiar but is seen in a different light in many Byzantine icons and theology. The context is the pilgrimage to Jerusalem for the feast of Passover, the telling of the pivotal story of liberation of the people from bondage in Egypt, and the making of a collection of tribes into the chosen people of the faithful God Yahweh. Jesus is twelve, the time of coming of age in the Jewish community when he would freely accept the mantle of the Jewish heritage, law, and hopes. We are told very little in the text, but there is much written underneath the text:

> After the festival was over, they returned, but the boy Jesus remained in Jerusalem and his parents did not know it.
>
> They thought he was in the company and after walking the whole day they looked for him among their relatives and friends. As they did not find him, they went back to Jerusalem searching for him, and on the third day they found him

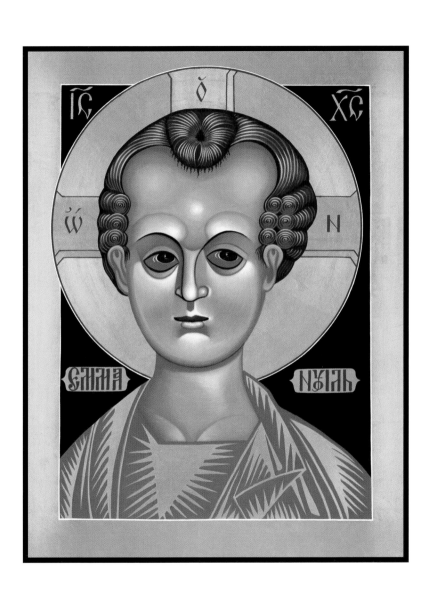

in the Temple, sitting among the teachers, listening to them and asking questions. And all the people were amazed at his understanding and his answers. (Luke 2:43–47)

This is the child that Luke describes earlier in his narrative, when Mary and Joseph have been to the temple after the birth of the child and have done all that is required of them in the law. They return home to Nazareth in Galilee, and "there the child grew in stature and strength and was filled with wisdom: the grace of God was upon him" (Luke 2:39–40). The child has been maturing, learning, and developing for twelve years. This is the child of wisdom, of truth, of the knowledge and presence of God contained within his mind, his soul, and his spirit — the knowledge of the ancients and the integration of tradition, inspiration, and experience of God. In Greek culture such a mature young person, discerning, questioning, and expressing knowledge beyond his years and study, is called *paidariogeron* — an old child. We are reminded that this is the Word made flesh, dwelling among us, in grace and truth for all to see, to hear.

This moment in Jesus' youth reveals what he is becoming for us and what he has been for all time: "wisdom from God" (1 Cor. 1:30). This is the learning, growing young adult, and yet he is also manifesting the wisdom of God, as it is maturing in his person. In the Book of Proverbs this person is described almost playfully:

> Yahweh created me first,
> at the beginning of his works.
> He formed me from of old,
> from eternity, even before the earth. . . .
> I was there when he made the skies
> and drew the earth's compass on the abyss,
> when he formed the clouds above

and when the springs of the ocean emerged;
when he made the sea with its limits,
that it might not overflow.
When he made the foundations of the earth,
I was close beside him,
the designer of his works,
and I was his daily delight,
forever playing in his presence,
playing throughout the world
and delighting to be with humans.

(Prov. 8:22–23, 27–31)

This is the person of the Trinity who took an active part in the making of the universe, the One who is in eternal relationship with God the Father, whose spirit is playful, creative, engaging, and like a child inquisitive, with always more to see, to enjoy, to declare "good," and to experience firsthand. This is both the young exuberant preexistent Christ of the Trinity as well as the youthful, exuberant Jesus learning, absorbing, and coming to appreciate the wonder and marvels of the Maker of the Universe.

This old child, overflowing with newfound, expressive wisdom, insight, and understanding, looks out at us, knowing us and probing into our hearts, minds, and souls with the same depth and intensity with which Jesus approached all of life and all people. His manner and his tightly curled hair follow the disciplined features of the Holy One. His deep-set, widely spaced eyes and his long nose and high forehead all indicate immense knowledge and wisdom that are as unfathomable as the ocean depths. The face is large, with the major portion found from the eyes to the hairline. If he were speaking he could easily be quoting the lines that follow the text above:

Now then, my sons [and daughters], listen to me:
happy are those who follow my ways.
Listen to my teaching and gain wisdom;
do not ignore it.
Happy are those who listen to me
and wait at my gates every day,
watching, close to my threshold.
Those who find me find life:
theirs is Yahweh's blessing.   (Prov. 8:32–35)

But this is the young Jesus, and his parents are concerned. We are told that they are surprised to find him in the temple. He is chided by his mother, "Son, why have you done this to us? Your father and I were very worried while searching for you." Naturally, they would not have expected him to stay behind, to learn, and to begin to try to express what he was beginning to know by the power of the Spirit that resided in him. Their being upset with him reminds us that he grew like other children, and yet there was within him the power of God. His answer sounds like that of an adult who has left home and is pursuing a life that is separate from his family and parental ties. He is bold in response: "Why were you looking for me? Do you not know that I must be in my Father's house?" But they did not understand this answer (Luke 2:49–50).

Emmanuel the Christ, the anointed of God, manifests itself as showing through the flesh of the young Jewish man with a sense of relationship to God that is as developed as that of the most astute of the prophets of the Old Testament. His answer reveals the relationship that is forming him in secret, day by day, year by year as he lives on earth, yet lives with God his Father. And his parents do not understand. We, too, do not understand how a child, struggling to sort out knowledge and learn prayers, laws, traditions, psalms, and the heritage of his nation and people, was integrating all this under the tutelage of the Holy Spirit and Wisdom.

But the time is not yet ready for him to begin teaching. He has much more to learn as a human child, a young man growing to be an adult in his time and place. He returns home with Mary and Joseph and is "subject to them." That in itself is a wonder — the Son of Wisdom is subject to human parents, humbly learning from everyone and all around him. And the Scripture continues with a one-line description that will encompass Jesus' life from this time, when he is twelve, until he is baptized by John at the age of thirty: "And Jesus increased in wisdom and age, and in divine and human favor" (Luke 2:52). This is the description of Jesus' apprenticeship to God, to the interior Spirit that formed him and taught him throughout his life.

But we are invited to sit before this person who is God-with-us and be apprenticed to this wisdom and holiness, young, playful, seeing all of history and the universe in the perspective of God, holding all things in his hand, keeping us alive in his mercy and teaching us throughout our lives. We need time, years of attending to the Word in the Scriptures, to the Word made flesh, to the silence and the eyes that ask us if we are looking in the right place, and dwelling in our Father's house and seeking the Divine in all the knowledge and information of the world. Those eyes remind us how little we understand and that we are called to be "subject to" God, the Logos, the Word, and the underlying principle of all knowledge: "All things were made through him and without him nothing came to be" (John 1:3). We are before God, and God is with us now.

6

Jesus Christ Morning Star:
Jesucristo el Lucero Radiante del Alba

Tell me, what is it you plan to do
with your one wild and precious life?

(Mary Oliver, poet)

This icon is something new in the tradition of icons, showing a
young adult Jesus, or Jesus as a teenager in contemporary society. This is a holy image of Jesus as a seventeen-year-old boy. For
William McNichols, the idea originally surfaced after the Colum-
bine High School massacre in Colorado, which indicated that the
world that our children are inheriting can be a frightening and mur-
derous place. And in light of the many experiences of death in the
last few years in schools around the country and in larger instances
of attacks on innocent people, as well as the number of suicides
among high-school students, the issue of death among youth had
to be faced head-on. Death can be perceived as a friend and/or as
an evil presence, like a stalker. Death itself is not evil. St. Francis
of Assisi once called death our "Sister." Yet the presence of death
as evil, in the deliberate destruction and murder of the innocent,
is also a harsh reality we all have to live with, especially young
people.

What would a teenage Christ look like and have to say to youth
in today's violent and insecure society? The young man is dressed

El Lucero Radiante del Alba

simply in his shirt sleeves over a T-shirt. The blue shirt is his divinity, the red undershirt is his humanity, his mortality. One hand is
over his heart and the other raised in the ancient blessing with
the ring finger bent to the thumb. His countenance is serious,
burdened, sorrowing, knowing life and death beyond his years.
This is sadness born of suffering and exposure to evil. And yet
there is serenity that is strong, inviting, and solid. This is someone to lean on, rely on, someone who would be a faithful and true
friend.

The background of sky is vast, troubled, filled with storm clouds
that roil and threaten. And below this disturbed sky is a ceme-
tery, with gravestones and trees stark against the gray air. But the
wounds in the hands draw our eyes, as much as the face of the
young Christ. This is the Crucified Christ, but risen from the dead.
He is described as "surrounded by darkness and bearing death's
wounds, but death has no dominance over the Lord of Life." And
that is why the icon might be named "I Am the Light of the Dawn"
or "The Bright Morning Star," from Revelation 22:16.

The icon is inscribed in Spanish because it was painted in New
Mexico, using a local Taos teenager as a model. In Spanish the
name Jesucristo el Lucero Radiante del Alba almost sings with
hope, drawing the person forward out of the ominous landscape.
This icon is a magnet for those who find life brutal, terrifying, and
nearly impossible to bear alone. This is a Christ who will be a
guardian and friend to youth, the Lamb of God, slaughtered yet
stronger than death in love and obedience to God and in care for
the trembling people of the world.

An ancient prayer ascribed to Clement of Alexandria is called
"Hymn to Christ, Leader of Youth." It is image upon image
of power, of strength and immediacy, which this young Christ
embodies:

O bridle of racing young horses,
Wing of soaring birds,
Safe rudder of sailing boats,
Shepherd of the royal lambs!
Unite thy simple children
That they may sing thee praises
In holiness and clearness
With consecrated lips,
O Christ, thou leader of youth, . . .
Almighty word of the Father most high,
Invincible stronghold of wisdom,
Eternal helper in anguish and fear,
O Jesus, immortal one,
Savior of mortal men and women, . . .
from the sea of evil
dost thou pull out and save,
O fisher of men. . . .
We owe to thee who saved us
and brought us into life.
With undivided hearts
We follow the mighty Son,
A company of peace,
Who are begotten of Christ.
O holy, chosen band,
In unity sing praises
To God, the king of Peace![15]

In the midst of uncertainty, of terrorism, of guns easily procured, and of hatred and insecurity, this Christ stands firm in blessing and companionship. The morning star is always there; the radiant light of dawn does come, no matter how dark, cold, and lonely are the terrors of the night. Among all peoples of all nations, races, religions, and ages, God beckons, blesses, and dwells with us. This is the firstborn of the dead, comforter and protector of those whose lives seem tenuous and in danger, threatened by violence, lost among the many.

Immediately after describing the birth of this Star that heralds hope, Matthew's gospel tells a terrible story. Jesus was born under the brutal regime of King Herod, who lived in collusion with the Roman occupation. When the wise men come from the east following the star, Herod and the whole city with him are disturbed at the thought that there may be someone who would "shepherd my people Israel" (Matt. 2:6). Herod only knows the name of the town, Bethlehem, but that is enough. Furious, Herod gives orders to kill all the boys in Bethlehem who are two years old or under, thinking that he would find the one that would be the future leader. He fails to find Jesus, but there is a slaughter of the innocents. Today the slaughter extends long past two-year-olds. It seems that young people are particularly vulnerable. But the aftermath is the same: "A cry is heard in Ramah, wailing and loud lamentation: Rachel weeps for her children. She refuses to be comforted, for they are no more" (Matt. 2:18).

Still today there are so many destinies unfulfilled, so many lost and taken by violence and the evil of those who seek to control through fear and rage. But the young man Jesucristo stands secure in his power over death and his gift to all those who seek life, "life that is ever more abundant," and at the service of others in need of a glimpse of the wisdom and presence of God among us. Oscar Romero, the archbishop of San Salvador, lived under threat, and yet he learned by watching his people where life was to be found. He wrote in his journal:

God exists, and he exists even more the farther you feel from him. God is closer to you when you think he is farther away and doesn't hear you. When you feel the anguished desire for God to come near because you don't feel him present, then God is very close to your anguish.[16]

Jesus Christ the Morning Star dawns over our lives, faithful and ever present, having lived in a world that often saw a threat in the very presence of young people. He spent most of his life, his teens and twenties, hidden among anonymous people, and yet it was in those years that he grew and "increased in wisdom and age, and in divine and human favor" (Luke 2:52).

Let us pray for all young people as they struggle to grow and to survive with grace that they will know the divine favor of God close to them and even visible in moments when they are searching with great need. May the radiance of the face of Jesucristo shine on them, and may they find peace in his eyes and friendship. Amen.

7

Christt All Merciful

God's mercy is so great that no one can speak enough thereof.

(Thomas More)

This icon is found in practically every Eastern church. It is called "Christ Pantocrator" or "He Who Rules over Everything" or simply "Christ the Savior." This is the all-ruling Lord of the universe, and the icon is often found high above in the dome of the church. Sometimes the Pantocrator is seen as a stern figure, the judge of the nations to whom all will one day render an account, but the face of this Pantocrator is gentle and mild, filled with tender regard, meek in the ancient sense of the word as nonviolent and full of healing and peace.

On either side of the halo are the Greek letters IC XC, the first and last letters of the name and title Jesus Christ, and inside the halo are the letters for the Greek word for "The One." These letters form the present tense of the verb "to be" and so can be translated as "The Abiding One" or "The One Who Is." This echoes the response of Yahweh the Holy One to Moses when asked his name: "I AM WHO AM" (Exod. 3:14). This is the Word of God made flesh, one with God the Father from before time. This is the one that Paul praises and worships in the early hymn found in Colossians:

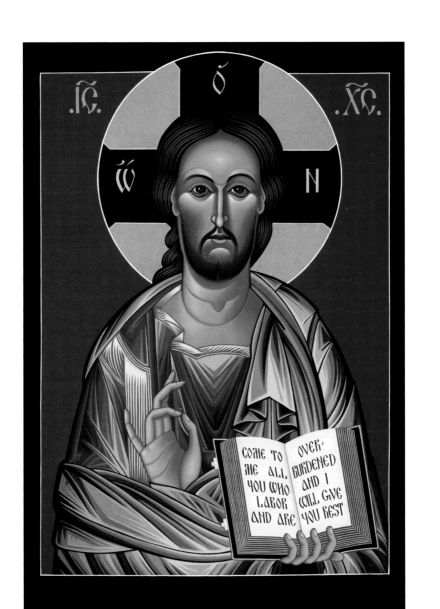

He is the image of the unseen God,
And for all creation he is the firstborn,
For in him all things were created,
In heaven and on earth,
Visible and invisible:
Thrones, rulers, authorities, powers....
All was made through him and for him.
He is before all,
And all things hold together in him.
And he is the head of the body, that is the Church,
For he is the first, the first raised from the dead,
That he may be the first in everything,
For God was pleased to let fullness dwell in him.

(Col. 1:15–19)

The power over life and death and the awesomeness of God reside in this icon, not so much in the body of the figure, but in the letters found in the inscribed name of God, proclaiming a statement of belief, and in the echoes of the letters inside the halo that refer back to Scripture. Icons teach, and this one teaches in letters and in the posture of the Christ — his right hand raised in blessing, the first three fingers separated, and the ring finger touching the thumb. This is an ancient traditional expression of the mystery and belief in the Trinity, of three persons in communion, and of the mystery of Christ human and divine who dies on the cross and is raised from the dead.

The colors of the robe also make this same statement. The tunic (*chiton*) is deep red, and the cloak or cape (*himation*) is blue, as vast as sky. Draped over his right shoulder is a piece of cloth like a stole (*clavus*), which indicated high status in the Roman imperial court. This person's power is revealed in his clothing, in his posture of blessing, and, again, in the book of the Scriptures that he holds open in his left hand. This is the source of the power, of the teaching, and of the mercy that are integrated into the very person of Christ All Merciful.

The book is open to chapter 11 of the gospel of Matthew. Earlier in this gospel, Jesus calls Matthew to be a disciple, to come after him. Matthew does and then invites Jesus to his house to celebrate with his friends — also tax collectors and public sinners. Jesus' disciples are reprimanded by the Pharisees when they question them:

> "Why is it that your master eats with those sinners and tax collectors?"
>
> When Jesus heard this he said, "Healthy people do not need a doctor, but sick people do. Go and find out what this means: *What I want is mercy, not sacrifice.* I did not come to call the righteous but sinners." (Matt. 9:11b–13)

The icon portrays Jesus in a full-frontal stance, facing us directly, almost as though he turns to look straight out at anyone who questions his actions, his presence with sinners and outcasts and the rejected of society. He bluntly speaks what the one who disagreed with him should know or remember — the teachings and the healings found in the text of the Scriptures. The eyes of Jesus — Christ All Merciful and He Who Rules over Everything — hold the glance that forgives and heals as well as the steady gaze of the teacher who reprimands and calls to conversion. This is the Christ who gives lasting peace, forgiveness to all who need it, drawing them close to him with absolution and blessings. And this also is the Christ who defends the sinner, proclaiming his message of forgiveness that we are to accept for ourselves and to give freely and graciously to all in our lives. This is the knowledge that is revealed in the book of the Scriptures — the inner wisdom that is sourced in the heart of Christ. The hand over the heart raised in blessing and the text of the book are a threshold, an open door, a welcome to all who feel outside, unwelcome, and are either reluctant to come in or kept outside by others.

The text is familiar and deeply comforting. It is a direct invitation to draw near to Mercy who is always standing right in front of us, though often we are blinded by our fear, our shame, our self-absorption, and our image of God that is at odds with the mystery of Jesus, the welcome grace of God, dwelling with us in word, in forgiveness, and in comfort. The words written are the words on the lips and in the heart of Jesus for all:

> Come to me, all you that are weary and are carrying heavy burdens, and I will give you rest. Take my yoke upon you, and learn from me; for I am gentle and humble in heart, and you will find rest for your souls. For my yoke is easy and my burden is light.   (Matt. 11:28–30)

Ah, this is a God that is human, reaching to embrace and hold, and a God that is divine, offering strength that never ends, peace that possesses one utterly, and knowledge that humbly teaches how to bear the yoke of life, of hard work and suffering, leaning on the all-encompassing power of the Lord of the Universe who also is the Mercy of God in flesh, word, and heart. We are encouraged: draw near, draw nearer still.

Margaret Mary Alacoque, who was devoted to this heart of Christ, writes prayerfully in her *Counsels, VIII* about this heart of Christ:

> The heart of Jesus is an abyss where everything may be found.... If you are in an abyss of dryness and weakness, go

bury yourself in the heart of Jesus Christ, which is an abyss of power and love, without being eager to taste the sweetness of this love until he pleases.

If you are in an abyss of weakness, of failings and miseries, go also frequently to the heart of Jesus. It is an abyss of mercy and strength. It will relieve and fortify you.

If you find yourself plunged in an abyss of sadness, bury the sadness itself in the heart of Jesus, which is an abyss of heaving joy, and the treasure of all, the delight of the saints and angels.

If you are in trouble and anxiety, the divine heart is an abyss of peace, and that peace will be communicated to you.

When you are in an abyss of fear, the heart of Jesus is an abyss of confidence and love. Abandon yourself to it. You will there learn that fear should yield to love.

Finally, everywhere and in everything, bury yourself in this ocean of love and charity, and, if possible, never depart from it, that you may be penetrated with the fire by which this heart is inflamed for God and man, as the iron in the furnace, or as a sponge cast into the sea and filled with its waters.[17]

This is Christ All Merciful. This is Mercy standing before us, looking at us with deep, abiding openness. This is the Word of God made flesh, Mercy in words, in blessing, in comfort, in forgiveness and peace. "Come to me all you who labor and are carrying heavy burdens and I will give you rest" (Matt. 11:28).

8

Christ the Holy Silence

Before Prayer

I weave a silence on my lips,
I weave a silence into my mind,
I weave a silence within my heart.

(Celtic Traditional)

This is not a common icon, but it belongs to an iconographical type that originated in the sixteenth century in Russia. Other images that belong to this group are "Sophia, the Divine Wisdom," the "Crucified Seraphim," and the "Seraphic Guardian of the Blood." All of these images share many of the same characteristics of figure and colors, with one or two details that reveal the specific virtue or grace and wisdom of this Christ. They are all young Christs, preexistent to Jesus the Christ, the Word of God made flesh in history, born of woman, conceived by the Spirit, overshadowed by the power of God the Father. That is one of the reasons for the wings. This is Christ who dwells in God and in the realms of the orders of angel and seraphim. He stands facing us but contained, with hands folded, crossed over his chest and heart. His halo contains an eight-pointed star, which, from the earliest days of the church, denoted divinity. And his clothing, his wings, even his skin and hair appear to be suffused with light.

This Christ is male (there is another in this collection that is

female) and is found in the tradition of the silent, suffering servant of
Isaiah. This is the Christ who is humble, nonviolent, freely picking
up his cross and laying down his life for his friends, loving his Father
and his friends in life, in crucifixion, in death, and beyond for all time.

And yet this is a Christ who stands secure before power and
whose very presence is Truth embodied and will not be silenced
with persecution, torture, or death. This is Christ before Herod,
before Pilate, before the Sanhedrin, silent, but in the Jewish tradition "silently screaming." This is the Christ who stands in solidarity
beside every martyr, everyone who speaks for the victims and
the innocent who suffer on the earth, beside every prophet and
truth-teller, knowing full well what follows from being convicted as
disciple and friend of Christ the suffering servant of God. Suffering
and glory are wedded in this icon.

Listen to Yahweh's description of Christ the Holy Silence in
Isaiah:

> Here is my servant whom I uphold,
> my chosen one in whom I delight.
> I have put my spirit upon him,
> and he will bring justice to the nations.
>
> He does not shout or raise his voice.
> Proclamations are not heard in the streets.
> A broken reed he will not crush,
> nor will he snuff out the light
> of the wavering wick.
> He will make justice appear in truth.
>
> He will not waver or be broken
> until he has established justice on earth.
>
> (Isa. 42:1–4a)

This is the Christ of John's gospel who stands in the garden when Judas and a cohort of Roman soldiers come to arrest him. And it is Jesus who steps forward and says: "Who are you looking for?" They answer him, "Jesus the Nazarene," and Jesus boldly declares, "I am he" (John 18:4bff.). This is the Jesus who stands bound before the high priest who questions him. And Jesus calmly tells him that "I have spoken openly to the world."

And later, when a guard standing nearby strikes him on the face, rebuking him to know his place, Jesus turns to him, interrogating him: "If I have spoken wrongly, point it out; but if I have spoken rightly, why do you strike me?" (John 18:19ff.). This is the Jesus who stands before Pilate, silent as others accuse him, looking for the sentence of death. And when Pilate asks him if he is a king, he answers truthfully, "Just as you say, I am a king. For this I was born and for this I have come into the world, to bear witness to the truth. Everyone who is on the side of truth hears my voice" (John 18:37b). This is the Christ the Holy Silence who can only speak the truth.

This is the Jesus of Matthew's gospel who, when arrested and brought before the Sanhedrin, is falsely accused, and when questioned by the high priest, "Have you no answer at all? What is this evidence against you?" remains silent. This is Jesus who stands before Herod, a king who was a lackey to the Roman empire, who piles question upon question on Jesus, but gets no reply (Luke 23:3–6). And this is the Jesus — hanging on the cross, being mocked by the people, the leaders of his nation and religion, and the soldiers — who is silent, crying out only to God.

The songs of the prophet Isaiah that are read during Holy Week reveal who Jesus of Nazareth, the Christ of God, truly is in images that are startling, horrifying, and bloody. This is silence that judges all who stand in its presence. It is the depths of one who knows

when to speak and when to stand mute witnessing to truth, revealing evil, sin, and injustice for what they truly are, resoundingly
without a word spoken:

> He was harshly treated,
> but unresisting and silent, he humbly submitted.
> Like a lamb led to the slaughter
> or a sheep before the shearer
> he did not open his mouth!   (Isa. 53:7)

Christ the Holy Silence is a martyr who speaks with his life, with
his presence, and his last word that shatters the dead silence is his
death itself. It is a statement that cannot be contradicted. In his
death, in his silence, is the fullness of his life. And this Holy Silence
is an ever-present reality for those who seek to know when to speak
and when not to, when it is not the time to defend oneself. Listen
to the Holy Silence in those who dwell within it or have known it
intimately. In *Meditations*, Dorothy Day says: "The position of the
Catholic Worker remains the same. We are Christian pacifists and
try to follow the counsels of perfection.... We may suffer for this
faith, but we know that this suffering may be more fruitful than
any words of ours."[18]

Or, look into the life of Catherine of Siena. In fourteenth-
century Italy, she spoke out about social issues, the care of the poor
and those who were afflicted with the plague, and about theological
issues, pleading with the pope and bishops to remember their calling, their responsibility to model obedience to the Crucified Christ,
and exposing the corruption of the church. Catherine had no fear
about correcting the leaders of the church when it was necessary:

> Now it seems that Highest and Eternal Goodness is having
> that done by force which has not been done willingly; it seems

that He is permitting dignities and luxuries to be taken away from His Bride, as if He would show that Holy Church should return to her first condition, poor, humble and meek as she was in that holy time when men took note of nothing but the honor of God and the salvation of souls, caring for spiritual things and not for temporal. For since she has aimed more at temporal than at spiritual, things have gone from bad to worse.[19]

When she was summoned to Rome, she quietly told Pope Urban VI to his face: "The world is lost through silence." She knew Christ the Holy Silence, and she knew that what silences was deadly and dishonest. In *The Way of the Saints: Prayers, Practices, and Meditations*, Tom Cowan proposes observing her feast day (April 29) by seeking silence, which nurtures faith and brings inner strength. "When you find yourself in situations where you know you must speak up, feel that encouraging presence of silence around you, and don't be afraid to say what you know is the truth."[20]

We stand and pray before Christ the Holy Silence, and we are reminded of our baptisms in an ancient prayer of the church:

> You are standing in front of God
> and in the presence of the hosts of angels.
> The Holy Spirit is about to impress his seal
> on each of your souls.
> You are about to be pressed into the service
> of the great king.[21]

We must stand still, stay there and let the Holy Silence of God seep deep into our minds, souls, and hearts so that our lives and actions are saturated with this truth, this holy silence and courage.

9

Jesus Christ Extreme Humility

We have come to recognize that concealed in the very fact of Jesus being ineffectual and weak lies the mystery of genuine Christian teaching. The meaning of the resurrection . . . is unthinkable if separated from the fact of his being ineffectual and weak. A person begins to be a follower of Jesus only by accepting the risk of becoming himself one of the powerless people in this visible world.

(Shusaku Endo)

During the late Middle Ages, the sacred Shroud of Turin, with a full-length "divine impression" of Christ in the tomb, was on display and held a great attraction for tourists and pilgrims. The shroud was apparently rolled up half way so that all that was seen was the head and torso coming out of the relic box. It seems that people and artists from all over the world were inspired by viewing the shroud and left with this image burned into their souls. This is probably the origin of all the icons of the dead Christus the King of Glory, Jesus Christ Extreme Humility.

(From notes of the iconographer, William Hart McNichols)

Jesus is dead. He has just given "a loud cry, 'Father, into your hands I commend my spirit.' And saying that, he gave up his spirit" (Luke 23:46). This is the face of Jesus in the immediate moments after he has died and has been taken down from the cross, his gibbet of execution and bed of torture, exposed publicly before the gaze of

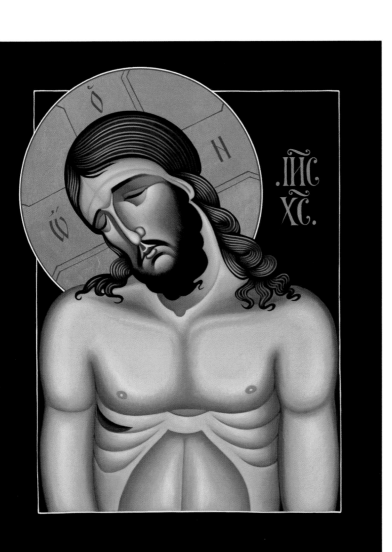

bitter and cynical people shouting for his death, inhuman in their lack of compassion for his brutally inflicted pain.

The body is slack, the eyes closed, the head has fallen forward, the limbs lie lifeless at his sides. He is dead, yet somehow his spirit still lingers in his flesh, holding his suffering, his prayer, his belief in his Father, his obedience, and his trust still visible for those who look and have the sight of faith and devotion. What did he suffer, not just in those last few hours, but throughout his life? This is a human Jesus, his body given in sacrifice. He was fully human and so would die as all humankind does, but he didn't have to suffer and die like this: shredded and beaten with iron-tipped whips, nailed through skin and in between bones to wood, stripped naked and exposed to a mob's hate. This is Jesus Christ, Son of God, Savior, Crucified, the Extreme Humility and the indescribable love of God for us.

This is luminous emptiness. And Paul writes to the saints in Philippi that this is the Christ we are to imitate and become before the world. Listen:

> If I may advise you in the name of Christ and if you can hear it as the voice of love; if we share the same spirit and are capable of mercy and compassion, then I beg of you make me very happy: have one love, one spirit, one feeling, do nothing through rivalry or vain conceit. On the contrary let each of you gently consider the others as more important than yourselves. Do not seek your own interest, but rather that of others. Let what was seen in Christ Jesus be seen in you:
>
> > Though being divine in nature,
> > he did not claim in fact equality with God,
> > but emptied himself,
> > taking on the nature of a servant, made in human
> >   likeness,

and in his appearance found as a man.
He humbled himself by being obedient to death,
death on the cross. (Phil. 2:1–8)

This hymn has sometimes been called the Hymn of the Self-Emptying God: in Greek, the mystery of *kenosis*. This is a man of pain, a body broken and wracked by torture. And yet something of the heart of this man is still impressed upon the flesh, and it seeps through, like a perfume that begins to fill an entire room, a house, and is released out into the world. The Greek letters haloing his bowed head remind us that this is God, the Maker of the Universe:

For God was pleased to let fullness dwell in him.
Through him God willed to reconcile all things to himself,
and through him, through his blood shed on the cross,
God establishes peace, on earth as in heaven. (Col. 1:19–20)

This is a life wasted, poured out, cast away in love. You can't look very hard or steadily at this icon. If you study it for more than a few minutes and let it speak to you, it begins to tear at your insides, tear open your own heart, and break down walls carefully constructed inside you. You want to weep, but they are only dry tears that make your chest ache and your breathing labored. This is Mercy's spirit leaving the body of Jesus. The only response is prayer, over and over and over again. Jesus Christ, Extreme Humility, sanctuary of mercy, dwelling place of divinity, have mercy on me. Have mercy on us.

Thérèse of Lisieux, whose name in Carmel was Thérèse of the Holy Face, used to say: "Look at God in Jesus, not just the child Jesus, but see face-to-face." When she spoke of being little, it didn't mean like a physical child, but it meant humble, as servant, invisible, lowering itself. She said: "The nature of Love is to lower itself," meaning the condescension of God, God's mercy in Jesus.

She would describe herself as being an "unpetalled rose," sounding to many as romantic and pietistic — but a rose torn petal by petal becomes nothing. What was cast off, thrown on the ground, wasted — that was supposed to be her life, her sacrifice. She was trying to say in other images what Jesus spoke of when he urged his disciples to follow him in humility. Jesus said:

> Truly, I say to you, unless the grain of wheat falls into the ground and dies, it remains alone; but if it dies, it produces much fruit. . . .
>
> Whoever wants to serve me, let him follow me, and wherever I am, there shall my servant be also. If anyone serves me, the Father will honor him.
>
> Now my soul is in distress. Shall I say: "Father, save me from this hour"? But, I have come to this hour to face all this. Father, glorify your Name! Then a voice came from heaven, "I have glorified it and I will glorify it again." (John 12:24, 26–28)

This holy image of Extreme Humility is what the surrender of Jesus to the Father looks like when it is given completely. This is surrender to all human beings, a life-long purifying process. And it proclaims that suffering can only be borne when the holy face of the Man of Sorrows, the one "acquainted with infirmities," is looked upon. The body of Christ, the Extreme Humility and Mercy of God in Jesus, imprints the mark of Christ's death on those who look upon the Crucified One and do not turn away from what we do to one another, what we did to God in the flesh of Jesus.

Peter Julian Eymard said, "Suffering is the seed of Calvary scattered over the whole earth." And in the first centuries after Christ, John Chrysostom asked his church: "Do you want to honor Christ's body? Then do not scorn him in his nakedness, nor honor him here in the church with silken garments while neglecting him outside where he is cold and naked." And Caesarius of Arles declared: "Christ hungers now, my brethren, it is he who deigns to hunger and thirst in the persons of the poor. And what he will return in heaven tomorrow is what he receives here on earth today."

The rich tradition of the church has reflected upon the sufferings and the humility of Christ and has demanded that Christians look upon the sufferings of "the least of their brothers and sisters" (Matt. 25:40) as Christ's own and do for them what our devotion desires to do for the crucified, shamed, and humiliated Christ. We must imitate this Christ of Extreme Humility in our dealings and relationships with each other. The only way to imitate this Christ emptied out is to obey the command of Jesus and to love, to practice the discipline of love toward those most in need, to tend to the bodies of the poor, the prisoner, the refugee, the cursed and outcast, even to "love your enemies, and pray for those who persecute, so that you may be children of your Father in Heaven" (Matt. 5:44).

A long, loving look at this icon teaches us one reality that changes all other realities, one illuminated by G. Carey-Elwes: "Humility is the truth about ourselves — loved." And the God that emerges within our souls is the God that is dying always to give us life, the life that is the relationship between Jesus and God the Father in the power of their Spirit. And that life has been poured into us with the poured out life and blood of Jesus Christ Extreme Humility. We can only weep, bow low, and turn to love back this God who dwells among us in the bodies of all who suffer, especially those who suffer because of our sin, our insensitivity, and our injustice in the world. Standing here before Jesus Christ Extreme Humility we learn to bend, to be humble, to worship in gratitude for such love, and to serve in response with humility all who are around us. Come, let us adore him.

10

The Passion of Matthew Shepard

Conceal yourselves in Jesus crucified, and hope for nothing except that all be thoroughly converted to his will.

(Paul of the Cross)

This is a contemporary and, to some, a controversial icon. It is written in the tradition of Jesus Christ Extreme Humility, a Christ crucified and dead. The body stands with arms at its side, looming large to fill almost the entire field of vision. The color is that of blood, of fire that accosts the one who looks at it. If one did not read the name above, it would be presumed that this is Jesus the Crucified One, seen in death with a background of a high sky and deer fence. But it is not Jesus Crucified two thousand years ago on the tree, gibbet of mob execution, all done in accordance with the existing laws and structures of the time and dominating forces. This is the crucifixion of a young man, Matthew Shepherd, who was beaten, stripped, and hung on a fence in a Wyoming field, and left to die. This is all too close in time and place, in the United States, done in the dark of night, in hate and viciousness and sin.

Oscar Romero, the archbishop of El Salvador slain more than twenty-two years ago, preached often on violence, for his small country was riddled with it, and he knew daily that it could spring past the borders of church or home and could take more lives. He wrote in one of his homilies:

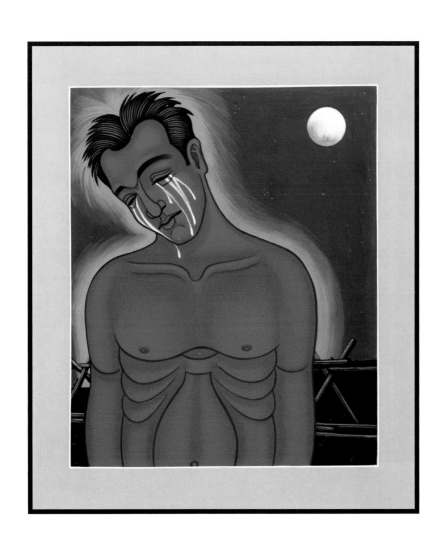

A Church that doesn't provoke any crises, a gospel that doesn't unsettle, a word of God that doesn't get under anyone's skin, a word of God that doesn't touch the real sin of the society in which it is being proclaimed — what gospel is that? Very nice, pious considerations that don't bother anyone, that's the way many would like preaching to be. Those preachers who avoid every thorny matter so as not to be harassed, so as not to have conflicts and difficulties, do not light up the world they live in.

A preaching that says nothing about the sinful environment in which the gospel is reflected upon is not the gospel.[22]

In the tradition of Orthodoxy, the one who "writes" an icon is writing the gospel, and so there are icons that cause distress by preaching the hard truth of what Jesus Christ preaches yesterday, today, and tomorrow. The icons of the first centuries caused much controversy and even violence among those who viewed them. The icon carries a power and a weight that can sometimes speak the truth of the Word more forcibly and shatteringly to the soul than the very Word of the Scriptures. But it is essential that the Word be written, spoken, proclaimed aloud, and brought to bear on the church in conversion and practice.

This icon speaks of crucifixion, of deliberate hate and murder, of rejection and humiliation of a group of people who are labeled "gays, homosexuals, lesbians," and so on. But the gospel simply states the truth: this is crucifixion and the murder of human beings made in the image and likeness of the Holy One, God. The murder of anyone is the murder of God, who point-blank declared in the gospel of Matthew: "Truly I say to you: whenever you did this to these little ones who are my brothers and sisters, you did it to me.... And these will go into eternal punishment, but the just to eternal life" (Matt. 25:40, 46).

And again Oscar Romero preached:

> We have never preached violence, except the violence of love, which left Christ nailed to a cross, the violence that we must each do to ourselves to overcome the selfishness and such cruel inequalities among us. The violence we preach is not the violence of the sword, the violence of hatred. It is the violence of love, of brotherhood, the violence that wills to beat weapons into sickles for work.[23]

The Word of God — in both the gospel and the icon — calls us to truthfulness, to conversion, to name evil for what it is, to repentance and atonement, to stop the evil, and to live in the midst of the world, as a community of beloved disciples who live with the light of Christ in all their relationships. Audre Lorde, a poet, essayist, and activist, wrote: "The quality of light by which we scrutinize our lives has direct bearing upon the product which we live, and upon the changes we hope to bring about through those lives."[24]

This icon is a light brought to bear on a reality, a terrible and deadly reality in our society. It convicts us. It stands us before Jesus Christ and before the crucified ones of the earth and sears us with the truth of evil, sin, and injustice. It says: Do not look away, but look. Look hard and confess. Do penance. And turn, turn toward your brothers and sisters in love, asking forgiveness, and then turn again to welcome them into the community of the Beloved Disciple. And then live a life of atonement by doing justice and living in solidarity with them and on their behalf.

As St. Augustine of Hippo reflected upon his own life, he wrote about what all Christians must remember and take to heart as they

stand before the face of God in Christ and under the judgment of
the Word of God: "Go in where thou wilt, He sees thee; light thy
lamp, He sees thee; quench its light, He sees thee. Fear Him who
ever beholds thee. If thou wilt sin, seek a place where He cannot
see thee, and then do what thou wilt." And the monk Bernard
of Clairvaux wrote: "It behooves thee to be very careful, for thou
livest under the eyes of the Judge who beholds all things. In all our
thoughts and actions we ought to remember the presence of God,
and account all lost in which we think not of Him." Our Judge,
our God's body, is each of our brothers and sisters.

This is the crucifixion of one young man; the only reason he was
murdered was that he was gay. He is the image of so many others,
so many groups of people, so many people whom others consider
"untouchable," sinful, disordered, as an excuse to treat them as not
fully human. In *Transforming Vision: Writers on Art,* C. K. Williams
writes on a painting, *Interrogation II,* by Leon Golub. Williams's
words could have easily been written about this icon:

1. There will always be an issue: doctrine, dogma, differences
of conscience, politics or creed. There will always be a reason: heresy, rebellion, dissidence, inadequate conviction or
compliance.

There will always be the person to command it.... There
will always be the victim: trembling, fainting, fearful, ab-
ducted, bound and brought here; there will always be the
order, and the brutes, thugs, reptiles, scum to carry out
the order.

There will always be the room, the chair, the room whose
walls are blood, the chair of shame. There will always be the
body, hooded, helpless; and the soul within, trembling, fearful,
shamed....

5. I didn't know the ladder to divinity on which were dreamed
ascending and descending angels, on which sodden spirit was
supposed to rarify and rise, had become an instrument of tor-
ment, wrist-holes punctured in its rungs, chains to hold the
helpless body hammered in its uprights.

I didn't know how incidental it can seem beside such im-
plements of pain and degradation; neither did I know, though,
how much presence can be manifested in the hooded, helpless
body: brutalized and bound, sinews, muscles, skin, still are lit
with grace and pride and hope.[25]

Since the beginnings of Judeo-Christian spirituality, the human
being has been considered the candle of God. A line from the Book
of Proverbs says it thus: "The human spirit is the lamp of the Lord,
searching every innermost part" (Prov. 20:27, NRSV). We are one,
body and soul, and what the body experiences the soul knows in its
deepest place. Our God became flesh of our flesh and bone of our
bone, taking upon himself the burden of mortality and embracing
freely our human condition, even dying with us. And yet our God's
love is deeper still. Not only did God die with us — he was killed
at our hands so that justice could radiate from the Father in the
resurrection of the body. Jesus' resurrection cloaks the whole of
earth with justice and wraps this mantle around the body of every
human being.

This icon stuns us with the truth of what we do to each other
and what we do to the Word made flesh that dwells among us.
And at the same time it paradoxically declares, "Love transforms
and divinizes everything, and mercy pardons all."[26] As in all icons,
it is the incarnation that is at stake, and it is the incarnation, the
Word made flesh, that is put before our eyes to contemplate and
take to heart. This icon reminds us that we are to look upon all

human beings with the tender regard, compassion, kindness, and love with which we look upon our God.

And we pray: Jesus the Crucified One, may your passion and death save us and turn our lives from violence to compassion, from hatred to hope, and from sin to light. May our lives mirror your passion, your forgiveness, and your mercy toward all. Amen.

11

Jesus Christ Holy Forgiveness

I want to forgive, I want to reign over souls and pardon all nations. My peace must be extended over the entire universe. . . . I am Wisdom and Beatitude; I am Love and Mercy! I am Peace; I shall reign!

My reign shall be one of peace and love and I shall inaugurate it by compassion on all. Such is the end I have in view and this is the great work of my love.

(Josefa Menéndez, twentieth-century Spanish mystic)

This Christ seems to be larger than life, to be coming forth toward us out of the frame of the icon, to loom before us. In the halo that fills and overlaps the frame is the cross and the Greek letters for "The Abiding One Who Is," naming this as the Christ who forgives us in his living and dying on the cross. These letters are one with the letter of Paul to the Colossians when he reminds believers:

You yourselves were once estranged and opposed to God because of your evil deeds, but now you have been reconciled. God reconciled you by giving up to death the body of Christ, so that you may be without fault, holy and blameless before him. Only stand firm, upon the foundation of your faith, and be steadfast in hope. Keep in mind the Gospel you have heard, which has been preached to every creature under heaven.

(Col. 1:21–23)

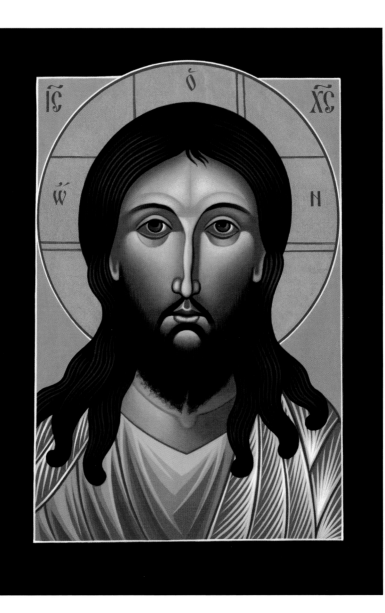

But this Christ looms like the figure of a mother, ever watchful of children that are absorbed in getting what they want, ignoring warning words and oblivious of the effects of their actions on others. Or, in the words of John Vianney, who was known for his gentleness and insight as a confessor, "God is like a mother who carries her child in her arms by the edge of a precipice. While she is seeking all the time to keep him from danger, he is doing his best to get into it."

Jesus Christ Holy Forgiveness is in essence the totality of the gospel, the Good News of God to all on earth. We are forgiven. We are free. We are loved. We are acceptable as friends to God. We are invited back to intimacy and knowledge of God. We are made whole and holy again. We are always forgiven, for God is giving, forbearing, forgetting, and forgoing of even justice if, and it is a very large IF, if we in turn forgive all for everything in our lives.

It is a line buried in the midst of the Jesus Prayer, the Our Father: Forgive us our debt as we forgive those who are in debt to us. It seems simple enough. There are two words for debt used in that sentence that are lost in the English translation. The first debt is beyond counting, larger than the U.S. national debt, which stands at more than 570 trillion dollars. We ask for forgiveness for not being human, for not living up to the mark of being Christian, of being the beloved children of God; for all the evil, injustice, killing, and destruction of other human beings and the earth that has ever been done; for being in opposition to God; for not surrendering and worshiping God alone, but becoming like gods ourselves. All that is forgiven, laid aside, undone. Then the second use of the word "debt" occurs — "as we forgive those who are in debt to us." And that debt is nickels and dimes at most, no matter what we see as the sin, the injustice, and the evil that others have done to us.

We stand alone before Christ Holy Forgiveness, and yet we stand trailing every other human being in the world, bound in one body, the Body of Christ. We are all forgiven, and if we grasp that forgiveness as a lifeline and a freedom ride then we must extend that same lifeline freely and graciously to all others. It becomes not a moment when things are redeemed or redressed, or a collection of moments, but a lifestyle, an attitude, and a way of being in the world, being with God Holy Forgiveness, being saved.

To stand before this icon and be seen for what we are, and not to flinch, or at least not to turn away or run, or hide or blame others, or to deny who we are, is the power that is seeded in this Christ. How to stand before Goodness? No one, not even the closest friend of God in this world, is beyond the need for forgiveness or the need to forgive others, personally and in a larger context of being part of humankind. And we must mutually help one another to forgive and accept that forgiveness, and so to live in gratitude for our freedom and our welcome back to the proximity of God. It is always a stance one takes alone and with others.

Listen to the words of John XXIII, as he received the last anointing before dying:

> The secret of my ministry is that crucifix you see opposite my bed. It's there so that I can see it in my first waking moment and before going to sleep. It's there also so that I can talk to it during the long night hours. Look at it, see it as I see it. Those open arms have been the programme of my pontificate: they say that Christ died for all, for all. No one is excluded from his love, from his forgiveness. . . .
>
> For my part, I'm not aware of having offended anyone, but if I have, I beg their forgiveness; and if you know anyone who has not been edified by my attitudes or actions, ask them to

have compassion on me and to forgive me. In this last hour I feel calm and sure that my Lord, in his mercy, will not reject me. Unworthy though I am, I wanted to serve him, and I've done my best to pay homage to truth, justice, charity and the meek and humble heart of the Gospel.

My time on earth is drawing to a close. But Christ lives on and the Church continues his work. Souls, souls. *Ut unum sint! Ut unum sint!*[27]

That is a prayer for forgiveness, the giving and receiving that are the end result of a lifetime of practice, of daily discipline, and of conscious awareness of need. Such forgiveness is a gift for others, binding and holding all of us together in Christ. In the words of Gregory the Great, hundreds of years before good Pope John,

When we are linked by the power of prayer, we, as it were, hold each other's hand as we walk side by side along a slippery path; and thus by the bounteous disposition of charity it comes about that the harder each one leans on the other, the more firmly we are riveted together in brotherly [and sisterly] love.

Christian life, in its essence, is a rhythm of personal and communal forgiveness, asking and receiving, being asked and giving, that grows into giving without being asked and not expecting to be asked, being mindful of God's mercy that is faithful even when we are unaware of the harm we do to others. But it is also remembering and encouraging each other that there is nothing that cannot be forgiven — nothing. For most of us, most of the time we need the basic practice of asking, of examining our lives and coming to the realization of how we fail, of how little we practice justice, love, or mercy. And, at the same time, we need to keep in mind the larger reality of God's forgiveness, always greater than our sin, or any evil in the world.

John of Ávila wrote words that should touch us when we are afraid or reluctant to ask for forgiveness: "No force can prevail with a Father like the tears of his child, nor is there anything which so moves God to grant us, not justice, but mercy, as our sorrow and self-accusation." This, too, is part of the process of being forgiven and being freed, and turning to restore and repair the world we have damaged.

There is horror in the world — murder and disregard for earth, air, water, and human beings. There is misery beyond poverty — torture and disdain for human life. There is injustice — racism, nationalism, a litany of "isms" based on violence, greed, and arrogance. In a word, there is sin, evil, and injustice in every human heart and life and in every structure, corporation, community, and international organization. Jesus Christ Holy Forgiveness sees, knows, and faces it all and absorbs it into his gaze, his person, and transforms it and us, who are sinners, into new creatures. This is the work of God, the reign of God, the peace of God. Paul tells us in Corinthians:

> The one who is in Christ is a new creature. For him the old things have passed away; a new world has come. All this is the work of God who in Christ reconciled us to himself, and who entrusted to us the ministry of reconciliation. Because in Christ God reconciled the world with himself, no longer taking into account their trespasses and entrusting to us the message of reconciliation.
>
> So we present ourselves as ambassadors in the name of Christ, as if God himself makes an appeal to you through us. Let God reconcile you; this we ask you in the name of Christ.
>
> (2 Cor. 5:17–20)

Stand and be reconciled with Forgiveness. Take and receive. Give and share it around. Be reconciled to one another; walk together again with one another and with God. God appealed to us in Jesus. Now God appeals through us. Forgiveness knows no bounds. It is born of God.

12

The Crucified Lord

The cross possesses such power and strength that, whether
they will or no, it attracts, draws, and ravishes those who
carry it.
(Henry Suso)

The cross is to me certain salvation. The cross is that which
I ever adore. The cross of the Lord is with me. The cross is
my refuge.
(Thomas Aquinas)

*This is a processional cross; the front side is after the early Renais-
sance master Giotto. The barren trees flanking the torso of Christ
are an addition to show nature's emphatic grief. In the beginning
of his Spiritual Exercises, St. Ignatius Loyola asks the retreatant to
sit before the cross and question the crucified Lord. I kept thinking
of those questions during the process of creating this image and so
it comes to the viewer as a 'talking cross,' the kind of cross with
which Ignatius, Francis, Claire, Bernard, or Julian of Norwich
could have spoken.*

(From notes of the iconographer, William Hart McNichols)

The initials at the top of the cross, INRI, are the inscription in
shorthand that Pilate decreed should be placed above the head of
the one to be executed: Jesus of Nazareth, King of the Jews (see
John 19:19). Written in Hebrew, Latin, and Greek, it has come to
symbolize the universality of the community that is birthed at the

foot of the cross. The body bears the marks of the nails in hands and feet, the three wounds, as well as the wound in the side that was caused by the piercing with the soldier's lance. When Christ's body was pierced, blood and water flowed out (John 19:34). One of the lines from the book of the prophet Zechariah is quoted: "They will look at the one who was pierced" (Zech. 12:10). This line is found in a description of Yahweh saving Jerusalem from its enemies, but also from defilement with other gods and all sin:

> I will pour out on the family of David and the inhabitants of Jerusalem a spirit of love and supplication. They will look at the one who was pierced and mourn for him as for an only child, weeping bitterly as for a firstborn.   (Zech. 12:10)

> On that day a spring will well up for the family of David and for the inhabitants of Jerusalem to cleanse themselves of sin and defilement.   (Zech. 13:1)

This seemingly simple description of piercing the victim nailed to the tree and looking up at him to see blood and water coming from his side is more a theological description of a larger reality than it is the recording of a moment in an execution, the moment at which the declaration of death was made. The notes in the Christian Community Bible explain succinctly some of the layers of meaning in this experience:

> *Blood and water came out.* The Jews believed that only through the blood of their victims could they obtain God's pardon. Speaking poetically, first John, then later the Church, said that from the open breast of Christ came forth the sacrament of Baptism and the Eucharist, *water and blood.* From the cross, forgiveness and new life have sprung forth for us.

The open heart of Jesus invites us to discover the powerful, hidden and mysterious love that inspired his life. The disciples of Jesus, who had lived with him, would find that their memories and emotions would be diluted and disappear with time; they would discover, on the other hand, that there had been no word, or deed or even silence of Jesus which had not been an expression of his love for God. From his open heart on the cross originates the devotion to the Heart of Jesus. Let us not get distracted by intellectual ideas in an attempt to explain or interpret faith; rather, let us contemplate God's love and allow it to transform us, making us like unto him.[28]

The wood of the cross is black on beige on black, and the addition of the barren trees adds to the starkness of the backdrop. The body of Christ with its wounds running with blood seems so alive. And even though this is crucifixion, a man stretched inhumanly and nailed up, this Christ almost seems to fly, or to hang suspended in the air, hovering before our eyes. The image evokes the hymn of Wisdom found in the Book of Sirach.

He created me from the beginning, before time began, and I will never cease to be, I celebrate in his presence the liturgy of his Holy Dwelling and this is why I settled in Zion.

The Lord let me rest in his beloved city and Jerusalem is the heart of my kingdom. I took root in the people God has favored, in the land of the Lord, in their inheritance.

I grew like a cedar in Lebanon, as the cypress on Mount Hermon.

I grew like the palm trees in Engedi and the rosebuds of Jericho; as a magnificent olive on the plains and like a plane tree I grew tall. . . .

I spread out my branches like a vine; these are Glory and Grace. As a vine I put out graceful shoots and my blossoms are riches and glory.

Come to me, you who desire me and take your fill of my fruits. To experience me is sweeter than honey and to possess me sweeter than any honeycomb. Those who eat me will hunger still; those who drink me will thirst for more. Those who obey me will not be put to shame; those who serve me will not fall into sin.   (Sir. 24:9–22)

This image of the tree is laced and entwined from the Book of Genesis through the Prophets. The Book of Proverbs says in one line: "The fruit of the upright is a tree of life" (Prov. 11:30a). And the prophet Ezekiel uses the images of trees to talk of the one who will come, who will establish a universal kingdom:

Thus says Yahweh: "At the top of the cedar I will take one of its uppermost branches, a tender twig and plant it. On a lofty, massive mountain, on a high mountain of Israel I will plant it. It will produce branches and bear fruit and become a magnificent cedar. Birds of all kinds will nest in it and find shelter in its branches. And all the trees of the field shall know that I am Yahweh, I who bring down the lofty tree and make the lowly tree tall. I will make the tree that is full of sap wither and the dry tree bloom. I, Yahweh, have spoken and this will I do.   (Ezek. 17:22–24)

The cross is the new Tree of Life that was lost to humankind in the Garden of Eden. Now, again, paradise is open and life is given back to us in a promise of resurrection. The entire book of the Scriptures begins and ends in gardens, with us standing at the foot of trees and looking up into them. Revelation ends with a dream that is a promise still to come true:

> Then he showed me the river of life, clear as crystal, gushing from the throne of God and of the Lamb. In the middle of the city, on both sides of the river are the trees of life producing fruit twelve times, once each month, the leaves of which are for the healing of nations.
>
> No longer will there be a curse; the throne of God and of the Lamb will be in the city and God's servants will live in his presence. They will see his face and his name will be on their foreheads. There will be no more night. They will not need the light of lamp or sun for God himself will be their light and they will reign forever. (Rev. 22:1–5)

We are summoned to stand before the cross and to contemplate the fullness of life, the person of the dying Christ Crucified who hangs before us. This is testimony against our violence and inhumanity and, paradoxically, a silent statement of the power of nonviolent love over injustice and death. God will die. God has died. God suffers and dies bound to us in flesh and blood, but while we seek to kill, our God is the God of life and will not let us remain deadened and fruitless. The Crucified One is before our eyes always like a mirror if only we would "look upon the one whom we have pierced."

Since Good Friday the cross and the Crucified One have formed the basis of the belief that love, forgiveness, justice, and mercy are stronger than death, evil, hatred, and killing, and that everything, even suffering and death, is redeemable in the wisdom and power of the God of life reaching out to us in Jesus Christ Crucified.

In the early centuries of the church, Justin Martyr wrote:

Consider whether the business of the world could be carried on without the figure of the cross. The sea cannot be crossed until this sign of victory, the mast, remains upright. Without it there would be no ploughing, nor could diggers or mechanics do their work without cross-shaped tools. Humans are distinguished from beasts by their upright posture and the way they can extend their arms. The very nose through which we get our breath is set at right angles to the brow, fulfilling the prophet's words: "Our Lord Christ is the breath before our face."

Consider Christ Crucified. Evil is overcome by the one who is nailed to a tree. Consider Christ Crucified. Wisdom is given in looking upon the Tree of Life, upon the dying Christ. Consider Christ Crucified. This is love, the love of God for all that has been made, and our God will not let us succumb to evil and to everlasting death. John Vianney writes: "To be loved by God, to be united to God, to live in the Presence of God, to live for God! Oh! How wonderful life is — and death!" And let us pray in the tradition of the Byzantine liturgy:

Lord, nailed to the cross,
at your sight the sun lost its brightness,
the veil of the temple was torn,
the earth trembled, the rocks split apart,
not being able to bear the sight of the Creator
unjustly suffering upon the tree
and insulted by the wicked. . . .
The tree of your cross, Christ God,
has become the tree of life for those who believe.
By it, defeating the power of death,
you have given us life, who were dead through our sins.

Therefore we cry to you:
Lord, strength of the universe, glory to you!

Christ God,
you have wrought salvation in the midst of the earth,
you have stretched out your most pure arms on the cross,
reuniting all peoples who cry out:
glory to you, O Lord!

Consider Christ Crucified. Amen.

13

The Risen Christ

For peace comes dropping slow
dropping from the veils of morning.

(W. B. Yeats)

This is the Risen Lord, standing as Lord for all time, in all places. He stands bearing the wounds of his passion and death, his devotion and obedience and love. And he stands greeting us with open arms amid the blue mandala of eternity. This is the One that the just man Job cried out to in belief: "For I know that my Redeemer lives and that he, the last, will take his stand on earth" (Job 19:25). This is the One who is the fullness of life, of truth, the Word made flesh, crucified and risen. This is the fullness of the prophecies, the One written about in Scriptures, the Christ who would suffer before entering into his glory.

On the road to Emmaus this Risen Christ is veiled, hidden from the eyes of those who are leaving Jerusalem and their hopes behind them. Jesus walks with them and questions them about their belief and their lack of belief, saying: "What is this you are talking about?" They answer: "It is about Jesus of Nazareth. He was a prophet, you know, mighty in word and deed before God and the people. But the chief priests and our rulers sentenced him to death. They handed him over to be crucified. We had hoped that he would redeem Israel" (Luke 24:19–20).

They are restrained from seeing him. In their loss, in his death,

they are bereft and cannot see anything but their dreams shattered and their lives disconnected from any meaning. They state their belief and how limited it is: a man, a prophet sentenced to death. That's all. It is not enough. They continue to speak about a "vision of angels who told them [the women at the tomb] that Jesus was alive" (Luke 24:23). But they left and headed back toward their old lives. Anything beyond death, was, of course, impossible.

And Jesus begins, chiding them for their lack of understanding, their avoidance of the Scriptures that revealed so much about him, if they read them with faith, with hope in the promises of God's Word. He becomes teacher, guide, light of the Spirit, truth-teller, and revelation incarnate, distilling the darkness that clouds their minds and stunts their belief:

> He said to them, "How dull you are, how slow of understanding! You fail to believe the message of the prophets. Is it not written that the Christ should suffer all this and then enter his glory?" Then starting with Moses and going through the prophets, he explained to them everything in the Scripture concerning himself.   (Luke 24:25–27)

This Risen Christ still hidden from their inner sight opens the Scriptures, casting his light, his truth, and his interpretation on the Word. This is the Word made flesh preaching and teaching the Word of God. And he fills all things with his light, his understanding, gathering all of history, all of the prophets, and the story of liberation and freedom from Egypt's bondage and the promises into himself. But the road draws to a close. Dusk and dark come on. They urge him to come in with them and he accepts. It is he who sits at the table and welcomes them. In the breaking of the bread they see. But it is a flash of recognition and he is gone. Only then do they know what has happened to them. They speak in terms of awe and knowledge now: "Were not our hearts filled with ardent yearning when he was talking to us on the road and explaining the Scriptures?" (Luke 24:32).

They rush back to Jerusalem and meet all the others who have heard the word about the Risen Christ. They share their stories of the Word made flesh, crucified, and risen from death and alive, and as they speak, "Jesus himself stood in their midst. (And he said to them, 'Peace to you')" (Luke 24:36). It seems speaking in faith, in hope, and in ardent passionate longing for the Word calls forth the presence of the Word made flesh in their midst. And after they have gotten over their fright, and he has eaten some fish, he begins to teach them as a group, as his community, again chiding them for their lack of understanding, their blindness in reading the Word of God, in leaving out the suffering and so missing the underlying foundation of the power of God in resurrection. He instructs them, and then he commissions them with his life's work:

> Then Jesus said to them, "Remember the words I spoke to you when I was still with you: Everything written about me in the Law of Moses, the Prophets and the Psalms had to be fulfilled." Then he opened their minds to understand the Scriptures.
>
> And he went on, "You see what was written: the Messiah had to suffer and on the third day rise from the dead. Then repentance and forgiveness in his name would be proclaimed to all the nations, beginning from Jerusalem. Now you shall be witnesses to this. And this is why I will send you what my Father promised. So remain in the city until you are invested with power from above." (Luke 24:44–49)

They will be clothed with the gifts and understanding of the Spirit of God, the presence of the Risen Lord to remain with them, instructing and teaching them all that they must know. Just as this Risen Christ is clothed in garments draped in the colors of dawn and hope, they must be wrapped in the garments of God, wrapped in knowledge, truth, and understanding of the Word in Scripture, the Word made flesh, the Word crucified and risen, the Word of the Spirit, the Word of the Father.

This is the cornerstone and heart of our religion and faith, the presence of the Risen Christ that abides among us. From the earliest days of the church, believers have sought to put into words what this mystery might mean for human beings, for history, and for the earth itself. Words sing and yet they stumble. They elucidate and yet they are vague. They seek to express the inner light that is given to those who are baptized and come to know the Risen Lord in his mysteries.

This is a hymn by Hippolytus of Rome (around 236) about the Pasch, the Passover from death to life, the resurrection:

> It is the Pasch; the Pasch of the Lord....
> O you, who are truly all in all!...
> The joy, the honor, the food, and the delight of every
>   creature;
> through you the shadows of death have fled away,
> and life is given to all,
> the gates of heaven are flung open.
> God becomes man
> and man is raised up to the likeness of God.
>
> O divine Pasch!...
> O Pasch, light of new splendor!...
> The lamps of our souls will no more burn out.
> The flame of grace,
> divine and spiritual, burns in body and soul,
> nourished by the resurrection of Christ.

We beg you, O Christ, Lord God,
eternal king of the spiritual world,
stretch out your protecting hands
over your holy Church
and over your holy people;
defend them, keep them, preserve them....

Raise up your standard over us
and grant that we may sing with Moses
the song of victory,
for yours is the glory and the power for all eternity!
Amen.

And this power, this glory, this defense, this victory, this standard, this enduring presence, this wisdom, this person is PEACE. So many mysteries are gathered into the Scriptures and in the resurrection of Christ. This one truth holds all the others. This is the essence, the source, and the meaning of Christian life, hope and belief, of community, of liturgy, and of prayer. Always we stand in the presence of the Risen One, whether we are aware of it or not. Anthony of Egypt tried to say it this way: "By the word of His power He gathered us out of all lands, from one end of the earth to the other end of the world, and made resurrection of our minds, and remission of our sins, and taught us that we are members one of another." This mystery of the Word rising in our hearts will one day raise our bodies to glory. We stand, we kneel, we sit at the table of the Risen Lord, and our minds are opened to the Scriptures and our hearts are stirred to fire and hope again, always. Amen.

14

The Mandylion
(The Face Not Made by Human Hands)

Like the deer that yearns for running streams,
So my soul is yearning for you, my God.

My soul is thirsting for God, the God of my life;
When can I enter and see the face of God?

(Ps. 42:1–2)

This icon is traditionally the first that an apprentice iconographer writes to practice his eye and hand, because there are also traditions that this was one of the first icons. In the West, this icon is known as the "Holy Visage," or the "Holy Face of Christ," and in the East as "The Savior Archeiropoietos." There is an old legend attached to the image and how it was made and kept on earth, treasured not just for the image itself, but for the theological principle of the incarnation that it reveals — this image goes back to Christ himself while on earth.

The legend says that a certain King Abgarus lived in Edessa and likely suffered from leprosy. Word of this King Jesus, a prophet and healer, had spread, and he wondered if this Jesus could heal him. And so King Abgarus sent his servant Ananias with a letter, inviting Jesus to come to Edessa, hoping that he could ask Jesus while in his presence to heal him. The servant went and found Jesus teaching, but because of the crowd, he couldn't get near enough

to Jesus to give him the letter. He knew how bitterly disappointed his king would be, and he just couldn't return empty-handed, so he climbed a high rock and tried to draw a picture of the face of Jesus. But he found out that he couldn't because of the radiance shining from Jesus' face.

But Jesus noticed him trying to draw his face and called him over. The servant delivered the letter and Jesus declined, saying that he could not go to Edessa because he had to finish the work that the Father had entrusted to him before he returned to the Father. But he said that later he would send one of his disciples to Edessa. And the legend says, at that point, Jesus asked for a bowl of water and a cloth. He wet the cloth and then pressed it against his face, and the image of Jesus was transferred to the cloth. Thus it is called the image "not made by human hands," a likeness of himself impressed on a cloth, called in Greek, a *mandilion* — a true likeness. Ananias the servant took the cloth as a gift from Jesus back to King Abgarus. It was treasured as a relic, with healing power, and in the absence of Jesus himself, it had the power to effect wholeness.

This image of "The Mandylion" (not made by human hands) is also the word that is found often in the New Testament writings. The first reference is found in Mark's gospel, when Jesus is brought before the council of chief priests, who are trying in vain to find evidence to use against him that will validate their sentence of death:

> Even though many came up to speak falsely against him, their evidence did not agree. At last some stood up and gave this false witness: "We heard him say: 'I will destroy this Temple made by hands and in three days I will build another not made by human hands.'" But even so their evidence did not agree.
>
> (Mark 14:56–59)

The description of "not made by human hands" here refers in their understanding to the temple in Jerusalem that had taken more than forty years to build. In truth, however, it refers to the body of Jesus, the new temple, that will be crucified, buried, and then raised from the dead on the third day. In Paul's letter to the Corinthians, he extends this image, and what God the Father does for Jesus, to what God the Father will do for us: "We know that when our earthly dwelling, or rather our tent, is destroyed, we may count on a building from God, a heavenly dwelling not built by human hands, that lasts forever" (2 Cor. 5:1).

These references are important because they trace the development of belief in the person and body of Christ to the community of believers and how the Spirit of God in Jesus is shared and transferred to believers in baptism, healing, and forgiving, transforming us into the likeness of Christ. The legend says exactly what St. Paul says, that "with unveiled faces, we all reflect the Glory of God, while we are transformed into his likeness and experience his Glory more and more by the action of the Lord who is spirit" (2 Cor. 3:18).

In the legend, the making of an icon is linked intimately with Jesus, human and divine, the Word of God taking flesh and dwelling among us in the mystery of the incarnation. In fact, the making of icons can be seen as

> part of the manifestation of the Incarnate Word, an unfolding of the mystery of God revealed in Christ. An icon is thus the servant of the Holy Tradition of the Church, a servant of the Gospel, not a mere artistic device. Just as the icon painter must be faithful to the delineation of the image of the Savior made without hands, so the Church must be faithful to the Revelation given in and through him who is the True Icon of the invisible God.[29]

The lines from Scripture validate the icon, all of them repeating the depth and magnitude of the divinity of God that entered fully into our humanity in the body of Jesus as an overwhelming act of love. Paul Klee, the artist, said once, "Art does not render the visible; rather it makes visible." And so the icon makes visible the face of God. Or in more theological terms from St. Stephen the Younger, "I saw a door open in heaven (Rev. 4:1). The icon is a door." We are invited in to see the face of the living God by being in the presence of an icon, as we are in the presence of the Word of God, in Scripture and in icon. The icon is a testimony that goes back to the person of Christ himself and so is revered as is the Scripture text.

This icon has been described by theologians and those who have stood in its presence, learning from it down through the ages. Here is a more contemporary description by Agnes Cunningham, S.S.C.M.:

> As we look upon this icon, we are impelled to do so with a gaze that effects a simple, direct encounter with this Jesus who stands at the heart of our faith. We behold the luminous face of Christ, in whom everything that exists becomes light. In the regular features of this countenance, we find a grave, almost impassive expression that is not indifference but the absolute purity of a sinless human nature, open to all the sorrows of the world. The large eyes search the depths of our heart, even as they draw us again and again into their profound mystery.... The hair of Christ, falling in long waves, bespeaks time without end.
>
> Theologically, this "icon of the Lord on the cloth" reflects the christological teaching proclaimed by the great theologians. It attests to the historicity of Christ, it witnesses to his humanity, affirms the centrality of his role in creation and

redemption, and proclaims his divinity. This is the divine Person, fully and perfectly man, whose face marks him as the Image of the Father; he is the Eternal Word whose features remind us that he can resemble only one human person, his mother, Mary, the God-bearer, Theotokos.[30]

More immediately, the icon's healing power and transforming energy can be touched in veneration, prayer, contemplation, in liturgy and Word. The glory of the Lord is near. In the presence of the icon we are in the presence of the Triune God, and we, too, like King Abgarus, can be healed, restored, and made whole in body, mind, and spirit. For all holiness, all wholeness, all repair, and all restoration are found in Jesus Christ, the Son of God, the image of God made man. Jesus is the indescribable glory of God shining on a human face, and because of the incarnation that indescribable glory now shines on the faces of all human beings.

The legend continues. The servant brought the cloth back to his king with the promise that a disciple would follow him. The cloth was laid on the king's face, and he was healed, with most of the more serious effects of the disease erased, leaving only a few marks on his face. Later, the disciple Thaddeus came to Edessa and converted the king, and the king was completely healed of his affliction.

Always we are reminded that this is a human face. This is Jesus who "made up his mind to go to Jerusalem" (Luke 9:51). This is the brightness of the Father's glory. This is the truth of the incarnation. This is the Jesus who was filled with the joy of the Holy Spirit and said,

"I praise you, Father, Lord of heaven and earth, for you have hidden these things from the wise and learned, and made them known to the little ones. Yes, Father, such has been your gracious will. I have been given all things by my Father, so that no one knows the Son except the Father, and no one knows the Father except the Son and he to whom the Son chooses to reveal him."

Then Jesus turned to the disciples and said to them privately, "Fortunate are you to see what you see, for I tell you that many prophets and kings would have liked to see what you see but did not, and to hear what you hear but did not hear it."   (Luke 10:21–24)

We have seen and we have heard. We see and hear. And the corollary of the mystery of the incarnation is that God became human so that we could become divine, so that we could come to mirror the image of the invisible God and be that image in the world, in our bodies and words. Let us pray before the face of God not made by human hands:

> Source of all being, Light from whom all shapes proceed;
> reveal your holy presence and make us holy
> by touching us again with your life.
> May our spirits recognize your Spirit,
> may our words speak of your Word,
> may our hearts rest even now in the peace
> that is your eternal communion of love.[31]

15

Santo Mártir Rutilio Grande, S.J., con el Santo Niño de El Salvador

A fountain fed from many springs will never dry up. When we are gone, others will rise in our place.

(Bruno Serunkuma of Uganda)

Rutilio Grande belongs forever to the people, especially the poor of El Salvador. He lived with them, served them, ministered the sacraments to them, studied the Scriptures with them, sought hope and freedom with them, learned from them, and suffered and died with them. His life mirrored this statement by Louis Guanella: "The heart of a Christian, who believes and feels, cannot pass by the hardships and deprivations of the poor without helping them." His help was expressed most clearly while he lived with them in the Word of the Scriptures that reminded them in the midst of terror and persecution that the Christ, their Savior, El Salvador, had come "that they might have life and have it more abundantly" (John 10:10b).

He was their shepherd, a good shepherd who sought to live concretely the words of the Good Shepherd, Jesus. He lived in a time of upheaval and the rising of the poor to stand and defend their rights to survival and live with dignity and hope for their children; it was also a time of brutality, slaughter, and massacre of the innocent and all those who stood with them and helped them find their

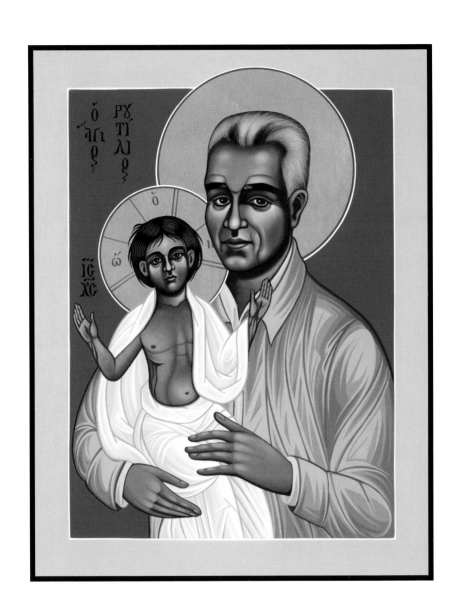

voice. His daily life of teaching, working with small communities, and preaching and encouraging delegates of the Word was rooted in the words of John's gospel:

> I am the good shepherd. A good shepherd lays down his life for the sheep.... I am the good shepherd, and I know mine and mine know me, just as the Father knows me and I know the Father, and I will lay down my life for the sheep. I have other sheep that do not belong to this fold. These also I must lead, and they will hear my voice, and there will be one flock, one shepherd. This is why the Father loves me, because I lay down my life in order to take it up again. No one takes it from me, but I lay it down on my own.   (John 10:14–18a)

And he did lay down his life for his sheep. One Sunday afternoon as he was driving from one village to another with an elderly catechist and a young boy, he was ambushed and the car riddled with bullets. He was brutally and cold-bloodedly murdered because his presence with the people gave them courage and aided in their growing more and more sure in their demands for justice. His persistent voice was one of the earliest cries that sought to be heard in the larger church and the nation of Salvador.

In this icon the priest carries and holds with tender reverence the beloved Son of God, the Savior, marked with the wounds of his passion — this old child, named El Salvador, has the features and color of the people of the country of El Salvador. In the 1980s, more than eighty-nine thousand people were "disappeared" or murdered in the country's upheaval and struggle for justice. The eyes of the crucified and risen child and the eyes of the martyr both look straight at us, questioning with clear-sightedness, a knowing born of death freely accepted and taken up on behalf of love, love for the truth and an entire people. The child's hands are raised in the

posture of prayer, lifted high, as they were both on the cross in
death and in blessing of resurrection. He sits as though enthroned
on the arm of Rutilio and comfortable in his embrace. And his
gaze is filled with wrenching sadness that carries the suffering and
deaths of so many of his people. They are heavily burdened, and
yet Rutilio stands holding El Salvador with the strength of faith
and dedication.

Rutilio's death set in motion both knowledge of the attacks upon
the Salvadoran people and the conversion of many to their cause
and defense. The most notable and probably the most exceptional
who was marked forever by Rutilio's brutal killing was Archbishop
Oscar Romero. It was Romero who prepared his body for burial,
aghast at the number of bullets that had ripped his friend's body.
As he washed the blood and guts away and dressed him for his
funeral, he was torn by the question of what kind of hate could
do this to someone and why his friend, whom he often disagreed
with on political issues, could draw forth such fire and threats by
his words and his presence with simple people in villages praying
and studying the Word of God. Rutilio Grande's killing catalyzed
the conversion of the bishop.

As he stood the next day outdoors, preaching with his voice and
hands shaking almost uncontrollably in grief and fear, the bishop
slowly grew visibly stronger as he spoke. The people said they could
see and hear the spirit of Rutilio seeping into their bishop and the
power of the Spirit of El Salvador emboldening and giving voice to
their hopes in their bishop's growing compassion for their sufferings.
The compelling love that Rutilio had for the outcast, the poor, the
peasant and *campesino*, the men and women of his country, was
taken up by Romero. And Rutilio's death propelled the archbishop
into the national and international arena, where eventually he too
not only would preach with his words and presence but would

be killed during a daily liturgy for daring to speak the truth to the government, the military, and the rich landowners about the necessity of justice as an integral part of religious practice.

El Salvador, the Savior of the world, the child of a people, a church, and a nation, appears before us as vulnerable and inviting, arms wide open, the upper part of his body bared and his left arm draped in the robes of burial and resurrection. He is crucified and risen, but he is so human, so touchable. He is the body of the poor, those hungry, jailed, tortured, left on the sides of the road to rot, daring their families to take them and bury them. He is the body of men and women who spoke up, as catechists and organizers, as ordinary people who helped one another in the face of danger and betrayal. And yet he is the Body of Christ, lovingly chanted in litanies of names invoked at liturgies with the resounding response of "Presente" — present among the people still and alive in the Spirit, summoning the people to courage and continuing work for justice and life. This child and this man Rutilio declare silently and surely the words of Dante Alighieri in *The Divine Comedy:* "These sparks, human souls, which come directly from God, have no end: they are imprinted forever with the stamp of God's beauty."

In the words of a fellow Jesuit, a friend of Rutilio's, this Child El Salvador, his body so filled with human pain, proclaims to all that God is with us, dwells with us, especially with those whose bodies know that same pain and death. Daniel Berrigan writes:

> In my tradition, an immunity system exists from the beginning. God is irremediably on the side of life, creates life from inert dust, cherishes life, finally sends an embassy of life, a very Son. A true blood brother.[32]

This icon reminds us that God considers us precious, holds us dear, and refuses to allow the ravages of hate and murder to prevail.

Instead, our God, Christ the Savior, is most easily found among those who are considered expendable to the great ones of the earth. Our God has decided once and for all in Jesus to dwell among these poorest and most vulnerable of his children. Today those who aspire to be saints of God must be the friends of these children of God and prefer their company and service to all others. And we must believe that this Child El Salvador is both Savior and judge of all the nations on earth and that justice will come as we pray "your kingdom come, your will be done on earth as it is in heaven." Clement of Alexandria writes:

> Through him all is one, through him is eternity.
> We are all his members; all ages are his glory.
> To Goodness, to Beauty, to Wisdom,
> To the Just One, all. To him be glory, now and for all ages.

16

Hagia Hesychia:
Jesus Christ Redeemer Holy Silence

For me, prayer means launching out of the heart toward God; it means lifting up one's eyes, quite simply to Heaven, a cry of grateful love from the crest of joy or the trough of despair; it's a vast, supernatural force which opens out my heart, and binds me close to Jesus. (Thérèse of Lisieux)

This icon is derived from the Russian tradition with an allegorical representation of Christ as feminine — Hagia Sophia or Holy Wisdom. The earliest known image of the feminine Holy Wisdom is found in a fourteenth-century manuscript from Mt. Sinai. The enigmatic aura of this icon, which grows with silent meditation, greatly contributes to its drawing power.

(From notes of the iconographer, William Hart McNichols)

There is a line in the Book of Proverbs that perhaps can begin to introduce us to this image of Jesus Holy Silence: "Say to Wisdom: 'You are my sister,' and call insight your intimate Friend" (Prov. 7:4). And another, from Miriam Makeba, that can startle us into seeing and being present to this icon in an altogether different way than reading about Wisdom: "I have never been to a university, but I do have common sense. I got it from my mother's breast."[33]

Wisdom and Silence are somehow twin sisters, not identical, but closely resembling each other. Both give a perspective on life —

121

God's perspective on earth, time, relationships, justice, evil, nations, structures, even theology and prayer. They invite us into God's provenance where all and everything have a seamless integration, and all is made holy and transformed, including us. When we sit at Wisdom's feet, we are of necessity silent. Our minds and our hearts slow down. We are stilled, "like a weaned child on its mother's lap; like a contented child is my soul" (Ps. 131:2). And in that stillness we are taught, beyond words, underneath and through words' deeper meanings. This knowledge, this wisdom, is spoken about in the psalms as being able to be "tasted" as well as "seen":

> I will bless the Lord all my days;
> his praise will be ever on my lips.
> My soul makes its boast in the Lord;
> let the lowly hear and rejoice.
>
> Oh, let us magnify the Lord,
> together let us glorify his name!
> I sought the Lord, and he answered me;
> from all my fears he delivered me.
>
> They who look to him are radiant with joy,
> their faces never clouded with shame.
> When the poor cry out, the Lord hears
> And saves them from distress....
> Oh, see and taste the goodness of the Lord!
> Blessed is the one who finds shelter in him!
>
> (Ps. 34:2–7, 9)

The psalms continually reveal God, Holy Wisdom teaching and revealing insight to the one who prays, either crying out in distress or seeking understanding. "I know you desire truth in the heart, teach me wisdom in my inmost being" (Ps. 51:8). And:

How difficult it is to grasp your thoughts, O God!
Their number cannot be counted.
If I tried to do so, they would outnumber the sands;
I am never finished with you.   (Ps. 139:17–18)

The Scriptures tell us what happens to those who contemplate
Wisdom: "A man's wisdom lights up his expression — his stern
look is changed" (Eccles. 8:1). We also find that Wisdom is found
in unlikely and hidden places and that not everyone appreciates or
cares to be taught by her:

I have considered something else very grave under the sun.
There was a small town with few inhabitants. A king set out
to attack it, laid siege to it and built great siege-works around
it. But a poverty-stricken wise man was found, who by his
wisdom saved the town. No one, however, remembered the
poor man. So I said, "Better wisdom than heroism," but the
wisdom of the poor is despised and his words are not heeded.

The words of the wise spoken calmly are heard above the
shouts of a ruler of fools.

Wisdom is better than weapons; one sinner spoils much
happiness.   (Eccles. 9:13–18)

And in the gospels, all wisdom books par excellence, much of
what is said by Jesus, Holy Wisdom, is ignored, considered naïve
and simply not practiced. Jesus' wisdom is nonviolent in its re-
sistance to evil and filled with the strength of compassion and
forgiveness. In many of Jesus' collected teachings, such as the Ser-
mon on the Mount (Matt. 5:38–45), wisdom is a new teaching
that brings dignity to those who are oppressed and living in a culture of violence and arrogant abuse of power. Jesus often begins
his wisdom teachings with a line from older sayings and then con-

tradicts, or adds to, them in such a way that they are startlingly altered:

> You have heard that it was said: *An eye for an eye and a tooth for a tooth.* But I tell you this: do not oppose evil with evil; if someone slaps you on your right cheek, turn and offer the other. If someone sues you in court for your shirt, give your coat as well. If someone forces you to go one mile, go also the second mile. Give when asked and do not turn your back on anyone who wants to borrow from you.
>
> You have heard that it was said: *Love your neighbor and do not do good to your enemy.* But this I tell you: Love your enemies, and pray for those who persecute you, so that you may be children of your Father in Heaven. For he makes his sun to rise on both the wicked and the good, and he gives rain to both the just and the unjust.   (Matt. 5:38–45)

We still revolt when we read these words, often not even stopping long enough to reflect upon them in the presence of Holy Wisdom, Holy Silence, "the greatest nonviolent resister in history" (Gandhi). But Jesus' wisdom is practical and liberating. Jesus and his people, living in occupied territory, were regularly slapped by soldiers or others with more power than they had, slapped with a right hand with some force, on the victim's right cheek. It was the degrading slap of unequals. And one didn't dare fight back. Jesus' words open a doorway for response that makes the dominant ones think twice about what they are doing. If you offer your other cheek, the left one, it is very awkward for the person to hit you again. They would have to hit you straight on, as an equal. Most would not let themselves get caught in that awkward situation of having to acknowledge the other as equal.

The same situation would develop with the incident of being

sued for your shirt and then turning and giving them your coat as well. It would show the creditor up as grasping and insensitive to the obvious need of his debtor. And anyone who, under the law, could force you to carry his burden a mile would not know what to do if you wouldn't give it back and kept on. Where does thinking like this come from? This is wisdom born of the presence and the knowledge of God. Theologian Walter Wink says: "These statements are so radical, so unprecedented, and so threatening that it has taken all these centuries to grasp their implications."[34]

The Word of God made flesh in Jesus Christ, the Wisdom of God, is best and most thoroughly learned in an attitude of silent listening, openness to conversion and transformation, and in the presence of Wisdom herself, while at prayer, both alone and in the company of others seeking to be formed in the image of Holy Wisdom, Jesus the Christ.

And once we experience this Wisdom it creates or seeds in us an insatiable longing and desire to simply know God in Christ. All of theology, philosophy, spirituality, and devotion comes down to one thing: knowing God and becoming the incarnation of that Wisdom in our own lives, for others. All knowing leads to one source: Holy Wisdom. Ambrose wrote:

> When we speak about wisdom, we are speaking of Christ. When we speak about virtue, we are speaking of Christ. When we speak about justice, we are speaking of Christ. When we speak about peace, we are speaking of Christ. When we speak about truth and life and redemption, we are speaking of Christ.

This is the Christ of God that we are created to know for all time, for eternity, ever disappearing more deeply into such Wisdom and Silence. Many of the saints sought to describe their meeting with and coming to know and love this Holy Wisdom, Christ. Julian of Norwich wrote:

> I saw that He is everything that is good and comfortable for us. He is our clothing that for love wrappeth us, claspeth us, and all becloseth us for tender love that He may never leave us.

And John Vianney:

> The interior life is like a sea of love in which the soul is plunged and is, as it were, drowned in love. Just as a mother holds her child's face in her hands to cover it with kisses, so does God hold the devout [person].

Catherine of Siena:

> I can love you more than you can love yourself and I watch over you a thousand times more carefully than you can watch over yourself. The more trustfully you give yourself up to Me, the more I shall be watching over you; you will gain a clearer knowledge of Me and experience My love more and more joyfully.

Sit face-to-face with Holy Silence and let Wisdom hold you fast, and seep into your soul, stilling your mind and calming your body. Let Silence soften your face and eyes and let God fill up what is lacking in you. Sit and be made holy. Be still and know Wisdom. She waits for you to come and listen.

17

Nuestro Salvador de las Sandias

One day, I saw with the eyes of eternity in bliss
And without effort, a stone.
This stone was like a great mountain
And was of assorted colors.
It tasted sweet, like heavenly herbs.
I asked the sweet stone, Who are you?
It replied: I am Jesus.

(Mechtild of Magdeburg)

The Sandias form a ridge of mountains that run the length of New Mexico, north and south, and are the backdrop for the city of Albuquerque. Below them are the Manzanas (meaning "apple") and above, the Sangre de Cristo (blood of Christ) mountains. The word "Sandias" has a number of meanings — in contemporary language, it refers to the color of watermelons; in old Spanish, it means "fire at night." All the mountains are named for colors of red and rose, the hues they take on at dawn and dusk. That accounts for the hint of flesh color and soft pinks that form the background of the land behind the Christ, Our Savior of the Sandias. The season is winter, when the light itself is transformed because of the altitude and the temperature range. And often the moon is visible late into the morning hours and again late in the afternoon before the sun begins to drop.

The notes of the iconographer say that he was inspired by the

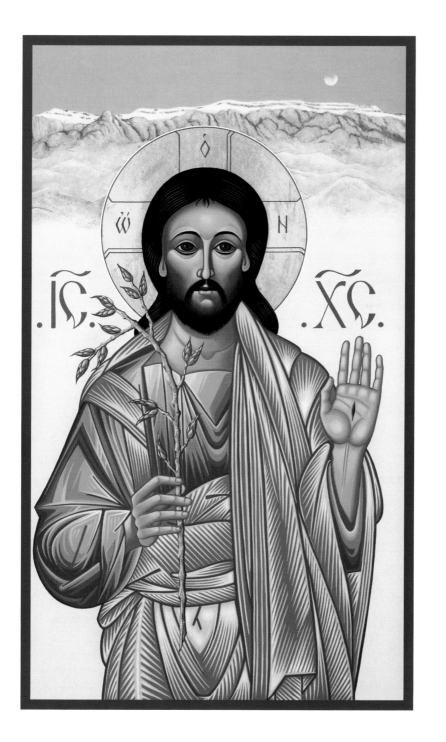

snow scenes in *Dreams*, a film by the Japanese master Akira Kurosawa. This landscape of fallen snow seemed appropriate as a symbol for the silence of death and the tomb of Christ. This is a Risen Christ, standing out against the shrouded mountains of early morning. He bears a budding cottonwood branch, one of the earliest signs of spring in northern New Mexico, where cottonwoods line the banks of the Rio Grande River. There is sense of a grave and deep abiding silence, as with snow newly fallen, as often happens in the early spring in New Mexico. These are the waters that will soon become wild refreshing run-off that the high canyon desert needs to bring forth crops and to provide water for the spring and summer months.

This is the moment of early morning when the suddenly gleaming promise of life is given again. It is like the dawn, running like poured honey, ever richer and thicker as it crosses the mesas and runs down into the valley floor, coating all the earth in warmth and new life. This is the seal of the Holy, the divine stamp placed upon the earth as the sun rises first over the eastern Sandias, igniting the smoldering ashes of old fires at ten thousand feet and then falling away to the canyons. With this morning light comes a peace that settles on the mountains. It comes at sunrise and then returns again at sunset with dawn and dusk fires. It arises in the east where the Son of Justice appears, the moment of resurrection when Hope breaks over the rim and runs along the crest. Light prevails.

This is the morning prayer of the mountains, the Sandias psalm song. This Christ Our Savior of the Sandias wears the deep adobe colors of the land itself, wrapped in robes that fall gracefully, a mantle of justice on the one who walks the earth again, risen from the dead. Along with the language of the old Spanish are the colors of Indian smudges, the smell of smoke, of sage rising, and of *piñon*.

This is the morning when all earth and all flesh need the touch of the Son of God risen from the dead to die no more. This is the soft radiant Day Star rising over us and our faces lit, made brilliant, blessed in this Son of God's forgiving merciful light.

This is the Light that Hilary of Poitiers in the third century sang of in a hymn. It is morning light, the light of day, light within light, the light of faith, light that breaks upon the soul and breaks into history with the incarnation and resurrection of the Word of God made flesh:

> O resplendent giver of light,
> like lightning at your command
> the time of darkness is past
> and daylight, regiven, spreads abroad.
>
> You are the true giver of light to the world,
> not as the tiny star,
> which, harbinger of the sun's rising,
> burns only with a feeble flame;
>
> but brighter than the fullest sun,
> all light and day,
> you light up the deepest sentiments
> of our hearts.
>
> Assist us, O Creator of the world,
> mirror of the light of the Father,
> for our flesh
> is fearful of losing your grace.
>
> And full of your Spirit
> having our God with us
> ... may the spirit preserve in holiness
> the temple of a body that is chastened. ...

> This is the hope of the soul in prayer,
> these vows which we offer:
> that the light of the morning
> may persist even during the night.
>
> Glory to you, O Lord,
> glory to the Only-begotten
> with the Paraclete Spirit
> now and for all ages.

The Savior of the Sandias blesses us and all of creation with his wounded hand raised in peace, in hope, and in a proclamation of the power of life over death. This is the Christ of the gospel of John and the resurrection appearances:

> On the evening of that day, the first day after the sabbath, the doors were locked where the disciples were, because of their fear of the Jews, but Jesus came and stood in their midst. He said to them, "Peace be with you"; then he showed them his hands and his side. The disciples kept looking at the Lord and were full of joy.
>
> Again Jesus said to them, "Peace be with you. As the Father has sent me, so I send you." After saying this he breathed on them and said to them, "Receive the Holy Spirit; for those whose sins you forgive, they are forgiven; for those whose sins you retain, they are retained."   (John 20:19–23)

This is the strength of flesh that stands against fear, absorbing it. Jesus died nailed to the tree, and his flesh still bears those marks. But it is the wounds that source the words of greeting, the words of blessing, the words that free. Peace be with you! Again and again the Easter proclamation is sounded, bringing forth joy, amazement, half-wondering belief — Can it be? And Jesus appears before them.

Now no place can contain him; no doors or walls bar his entrance; no fear can keep him from approaching us, bringing spring, the seed sprung into life with his very presence. All is transformed. Even the earth sings with the shadow of light that falls across it as he walks again upon the ground that could not hold him.

And we know in this instance of seeing our Savior of the Sandias that we are motes in the eyes of God, dust in sunlight. We are nothing in the face of such splendor, nothing but a flicker of air, a tremble of flesh. Kneeling is the only resort. Kneeling is the right posture to take, in the presence of the one who has saved us and now dwells with us until forever. Because of the resurrection, there are intimations of his light appearing mornings and evenings to remind us of "light from true light, begotten not made, one in being with the Father," the Light who summons us to life everlasting.

It is the time for singing in the land and praising God in the old ways:

> The earth and its fullness belong to the Lord,
> the world and all that dwell in it.
> He has founded it upon the ocean
> and set it firmly upon the waters.
>
> Who will ascend the mountain of the Lord?
> Who will stand in his holy place?
>
> Those with clean hands and pure heart,
> who desire not what is vain,
> and never swear to a lie.
>
> They will receive blessings from the Lord,
> a reward from God, their savior.
> Such are the people who seek him,
> who seek the face of Jacob's God.

Lift up, O gateways, your lintels,

open up, you ancient doors,

that the King of glory may enter! (Ps. 24:1–7)

Come, let us dance upon the mountains. May Our Savior of the Sandias lift our spirits and lay claim to our bodies, declaring his power over all suffering, all life and death. Our Savior lives and walks among us, light for our lives.

18

Jesus Christ Seraphic Guardian of the Blood

Where have your love, your mercy, your compassion shone out more luminously than in your wounds, sweet gentle Lord of mercy? More mercy than this no one has than that he lay down his life for those who are doomed to death.

(Bernard of Clairvaux)

The symbol or image of the seraph comes from one of the highest orders of angels: the seraphim, a shaft of flame, of light and searing truth. The individual seraph is a form of Jesus Christ Crucified. This image is found in paintings of St. Francis of Assisi, who has a vision of the seraph, Jesus the Crucified, when, in September of 1224, just two years before his death, he is seared, atop Mt. La Verna north of Assisi, with the stigmata, or the wounds of Christ. The icon is bordered with flames in the corners, making the image stand out more starkly. Traditionally the Seraphic Guardian is witness to all the innocent blood shed throughout time whose voice has been heard chanting since the death of Abel. The Scriptures speak of the very blood of the prophets crying out from the ground. And the Book of Revelation speaks of this blood of the martyrs who are witnesses to the Lamb of God in heaven:

Amen. Praise, glory, wisdom, thanks, honor, power and strength to our God forever and ever. Amen!

At that moment, one of the elders spoke up and said to me, "Who are these people clothed in white, and where did they come from?" I answered, "Sir, it is you who know this."

The elder replied, "They are those who have come out of the great persecution; they have washed and made their clothes white in the blood of the Lamb.

> "This is why they stand before the throne of God
> and serve him day and night in his sanctuary.
> He who sits on the throne will spread his tent over
> them.
> Never again will they suffer hunger or thirst
> or be burned by the sun or any scorching wind.
> For the Lamb near the throne will be their Shepherd,
> and he will bring them to springs of life-giving water,
> *and God will wipe away their tears."* (Rev. 7:12–17)

This Christ, the Guardian of the Blood, is the Crucified One called the Lamb of God, risen from the dead. This is the Lamb who cries out in the Book of Revelation: "Do not be afraid. It is I, the First and the Last. I am the living one; I was dead and now I am alive for ever and ever" (Rev. 1:17a–18). In a homily on April 29, 2001, Pope John Paul II said that these words of comfort

> invite us to turn our gaze to Christ, to experience his reassuring presence. To each person, whatever his condition, even if it were the most complicated and dramatic, the Risen One repeats: "Fear not! I died on the Cross but now I am alive for evermore"; "I am the first and the last, and the living one."
>
> "The first," that is, the source of every being and the first fruits of the new creation; "the last," the definitive end of history; "the living one," the inexhaustible source of life that

triumphed over death for ever. In the Messiah, crucified and risen, we recognize the features of the Lamb sacrificed on Golgotha, who implores forgiveness for his torturers and opens the gates of heaven to repentant sinners; we glimpse the face of the immortal King who now has "the keys of Death and Hades" (Rev. 1:18).

The responsorial psalm's refrain for the liturgy was Psalm 117:1: "Give thanks to the Lord, for he is good; for his mercy endures forever!" The Holy Father continued in his preaching:

Let us make our own the Psalmist's exclamation which we sang.... The Lord's mercy endures for ever! In order to understand thoroughly the truth of these words, let us be led by the liturgy to the heart of the event of salvation, which unites Christ's Death and Resurrection with our lives and with the world's history. This miracle of mercy has radically changed humanity's destiny. It is a miracle in which is unfolded the fullness of the love of the Father who, for our redemption, does not even draw back before the sacrifice of his Only-Begotten Son.

In the humiliated and suffering Christ, believers and nonbelievers can admire a surprising solidarity, which binds him to our human condition beyond all imaginable measure. The Cross, even after the Resurrection of the Son of God, "speaks and never ceases to speak of God the Father, who is absolutely faithful to his eternal love for man.... Believing in this love means believing in mercy."

Let us thank the Lord for his love, which is stronger than death and sin. It is revealed and put into practice as mercy in our daily lives, and prompts every person in turn to have "mercy" towards the Crucified One. Is not loving God and loving one's neighbor and even one's "enemies," after Jesus' example, the programme of life of every baptized person and of the whole Church?[35]

This mercy is the heart of Christ. This mercy flowed from the wounds on the cross. This mercy is the source of all Jesus' words, healings, forgiveness, and love. This mercy is the meaning of his life, his faithfulness in death, and his power in being raised from the dead to dwell upon us in Word, in Eucharist and the other sacraments, in community, and in forgiveness. This heart of God that is revealed and open in his wounds is an ancient symbol of God's and our innermost self. God seeks relentlessly after us, and our own hearts seek restlessly after God. John Chrysostom, one of the early preachers, wrote: "How should Our Lord fail to grant his graces to him who asks for them from his heart when He confers so many blessings even on those who do not call on Him? Ah, He would not so urge and almost force us to pray to Him if He had not a most eager desire to bestow His graces on us."

This image of the heart lies at the root of spiritual writing, of icons and of devotion to the heart of Jesus as it is sourced in the Scriptures of the death of Jesus. This place of the heart is where we live, where our souls, our deepest inner sense of ourselves, are simply always in the presence of God, whether we are mindful of this presence or not. John Klimakos, one of the ancient writers in the Eastern Orthodox tradition, describes what this prayer of the heart is like, in words, in attitude, and in practice:

When you come to stand before the Lord, let the garment of your soul be woven from top to bottom with the thread of forgetfulness of all those wrongs done against you. Otherwise, your prayer will do you no good at all. Let your prayer be completely simple. Both the Tax Collector and the Prodigal Son were reconciled to God by a single phrase.[36]

And that single phrase was "Lord, have mercy on me a sinner."

This mercy is like blood in our veins, like air in our lungs, like the ground we walk on and the water that is essential to our daily survival. It is mercy, forgiveness given and extended before it is requested. It is mercy that saves, that frees from the past, that converts in the present and makes a future that is possible and holy. It is mercy that sifts our souls revealing purity, single-hearted and single-minded love of God, and love of all men and women and earth, even and especially those we would label "our enemies." It is mercy that questions us as to the depth and breadth of our love in reality, in our actions in the corporal works of mercy, in our generosity and our forgiveness of others.

It is mercy that asks for truth: "Who do you pray for? How large is your heart? Who do you weep for, suffer with, and stand in solidarity with? Do you pray for conversion, your own and others, including the leaders in the church and the world? Do you pray for those destroyed by decisions of power, by nations, by harmful economic practices, and by racism? Do you pray for more than your own family, friends, communities, and country? What of all the innocents whose blood cries out to God? What of those aborted, killed by starvation, exposure, lack of clean water, no medicine, drought, and famine brought on and exacerbated by greed and policies of globalization? What of the innocent millions who suffer from bombing, landmines, invasion, and sanctions simply because they were in the wrong place geographically and found themselves to be another's enemy through no fault of their own? What of those killed, murdered, tortured, shamed, and disappeared because of their race, their religious beliefs, their gender, their sexuality, their "difference" from others?

This is the prayer of the heart, the cry for mercy, the presence of the Seraphic Guardian of the Blood who bears the imprint of suffering and carries the cries of those whose prayers were ignored in the ears and the hardened hearts of other human beings. We cry out for mercy, but do we return that gracious favor of mercy given to all who are in need of it now, here, in our world and lives?

Gregory of Narek (ca. 951–1010) wrote a prayer for mercy, a cry from the individual's soul. This is the prayer, though I have changed it to the plural form, to include all of us standing in Mercy's presence and in need:

> Good Lord, fountain of mercy,
> giver of gifts, Son of the Most High, Jesus Christ:
> have pity on us, rescue us, treat us with kindness,
> help us in danger, heal the wounds of our hearts.
> Bend over our misery,
> remove our doubts, and in the anguish that crushes us
> come to the aid of the weaknesses that lead us astray.
> Be as a doctor to us, in our sickness.
> Listen with kindly ear to our pitiful moaning,
> to the sigh that rises in silence from the abyss,
> to the cry of our limbs reduced to dust. . . .
> We trust in you, Lord Jesus, listen to us,
> you who alone are sovereign and almighty,
> creator of heaven and of earth.
> We await your coming
> and hope firmly in your mercy.
> We fall at your feet, kissing your footprints.
> We confess our debts, acknowledging publicly our sins. . . .

Graciously hear us, you who are full of bounty,
friend of humankind, forbearing and ineffably gentle,
day full of goodness and of endless light.
You alone can give to our souls,
even as they breathe their last,
salvation without end.
To you, with the Father and the Holy Spirit,
be glory for ever. Amen.

Mercy. Mercy. Mercy on your people, Lord. Yet, standing before this Seraphic Guardian of the Blood, we are exhorted to be God's mercy upon the earth, God's mercy in our words, our judgments and decisions, God's mercy in our touch and care of other human beings, and God's mercy upon our enemies. As the seraph touched St. Francis of Assisi, so the Seraphic Guardian of the Blood desires to touch us and make us, in our innermost hearts, the mercy and compassion of God on earth today.

19

Mother of God,
Soothe My Sorrows

Die! Die as the silkworm does when it has fulfilled the office of its creation, and you will see God and be immersed in His Greatness, as the little silkworm is enveloped in its cocoon. Understand that when I say "you will see God," I mean in the manner described, in which He manifests Himself in this kind of union. (Teresa of Ávila)

In any collection of icons on Jesus the Christ, the Incarnate Word made flesh, crucified, and risen from the dead, there must be at least one icon of his mother, the Theotokos, the God-bearer. This is the woman who bore the Christ into the world in her flesh, as Christ bore his cross to execution and death. This is the woman who bore the Word of God into the world as disciple, as prophet, as mother given to the church. She is the birth-giver of God and midwife to all who are born in his Word and in his water and blood in baptism and Eucharist. She is the Virgin who stood at the foot of the cross, lamenting the sufferings and rejection of her son — prophet, teacher, and Son of Justice. She is the young mother who stood with Joseph in the temple at her son's circumcision and presentation to God as firstborn sacrifice and heard the old man Simeon describe what she would become because of this Child, the long-awaited hope of all nations:

Simeon took the child in his arms and blessed God, saying, "Now, O Lord, you can dismiss your servant in peace, for you have fulfilled your word and my eyes have seen your salvation, which you display for all the people to see. Here is the light you will reveal to the nations and the glory of your people Israel."

His father and mother wondered at what was said about the child. Simeon blessed them and said to Mary, his mother, "See him; he will be for the rise or fall of the multitudes of Israel. He shall stand as a sign of contradiction, while a sword will pierce your own soul. Then the secret thoughts of many may be brought to light." (Luke 2:28–35)

This is our introduction to Mary's inner thoughts, inner heart, and the realization that she lived her whole life at the foot of the cross, both the cross that tore her firstborn to shreds in his flesh and the cross of the double-edged sword of the Word of God that laid her heart bare. She is mother to this child, but this child is the hope of the nations and the salvation of the world. And she is given to be mother to all the children of God who believe in this Word of the Father made flesh of her flesh and in the power of the Holy Spirit. Her association with this child of the Father will cause her great distress and put her in opposition to all who oppose the coming of justice and peace into the world. She too will be laid bare by his Word and work in the world.

In the icon she bears her child, burdened by his weight and size. This is not just a child but the God-Child, beloved of the Father, "in whom God is well-pleased, and takes delight" because of his obedience in becoming human and subject to death and in being the firstborn in the Spirit and in life eternal. She bears this child as heavy burden. She, like all Jesus' disciples, would learn obedience and become a disciple, picking up her cross and coming after him.

Her right hand holds her own head in her palm while the other hand is laid across his legs, not so much holding him as resting on him as he rests on her knee. She contemplates him, her arm embracing him in adoration, with distant intimacy. She is Mother of God, both human and divine, and she worships him whom she has brought into the world. But she, with all the children of the earth, is in need of his salvation, his Word, his presence, and his life and death, for her redemption and holiness. She carries him, but not only him. She carries all those who suffer and die because of their association with the Word made flesh, like her. She carries all those who will bear their crosses and come after Jesus the Crucified One. She carries all those who will seek the wisdom of this Child, God-with-us, as a sword of truth in a world of violence and injustice. She is lamenting what the children of earth will do to him and what the children of earth still do to one another, though in his birth, all became the children of God the Father.

She is marked with the stars of light, though the third star on her right shoulder is hidden by the light of God himself, the Son of God. Her robes are voluminous, the color as deep as dried blood. Her under-tunic is soft blue. Her child's clothes are the reverse in color. He is God made flesh. She is flesh made holy by God. Her eyes are deep and filled with sorrows beyond telling. She is looking inward and outward toward the eyes of her child, which are deeper still and old beyond all time. This is a formal relationship, a theological relationship. She does not support him as a mother would her child. It is he who is the strength, though the child is laid much as in a manger or as he will be after the crucifixion. He bears a scroll unfolded. He is the preexistent Logos, Word of God. He is not a child in the sense of years but is an adult man and God. This is the one written of in Revelation 22:16: "I, Jesus, sent my angel to make known to you these revelations concerning the Churches. I am the Shoot and Offspring of David, the radiant Morning Star."

This is also the God spoken of in chapter 8 of Isaiah; he is a force to be reckoned with and a warning. And there are the mixed and paradoxical images that are found in the prophecy of Simeon to Mary and in the text from Isaiah:

> "Only Yahweh Sabaoth must you hold in veneration, only him must you fear, only him must you dread.
>
> "He will be a sanctuary and at the same time a stumbling-stone, the rock that brings down, for both houses of Israel. He will be like trap and snare for the people of Jerusalem. Many of them will stumble, many will fall and be broken, be trapped and captured."
>
> Yahweh added: "Bind this testimony and seal it in the midst of my disciples."
>
> So I will wait for Yahweh who hides his face from the people of Jacob. I will hope in him. Here am I and the children he has given me. We are signs and portents in Israel from Yahweh Sabaoth, who dwells on Mount Zion. (Isa. 8:13–18)

This woman, this mother, sorrowing, knows the opposition and rejection, the pain and persecution, the suffering and death of all those who will seek to be faithful to the Word of God made flesh. She knows it in her own body, her heart, and she knows the pain that all those who are signed with the sign of the cross in baptism will know because of the world's reactions. This woman listens, hears, sees, and soothes, not stopping the pain, but sharing it and bearing it with him, and so, with us too. William McNichols wrote this prayer to accompany this icon:

Mother of God,
soothe my sorrows,
in this time of change and death.

Let me touch and feel
the guidance of the
bright Morning and Evening Star,
Jesus Christ Our Lord.

Help me to see the souls of the
innocent victims of disease,
violence and terrorism
rising into the light of His presence.
Amen.

She listens and is present to all in their sorrow, silent yet sooth-
ing. And yet this mother wants only the devotion of imitation,
as she obeyed and imitated her Son. We who know her as mother
must in turn seek to soothe the sorrows of all the earth, of the hundreds of millions of her children who live with pain and division,
with unnecessary death and sufferings. We must sit and look at
her gaze upon "God-with-us" and be drawn to respond with compassion, mercy, forgiveness, and presence to all those who know
the cross of Christ and who suffer in his kingdom for speaking the
truth of the gospel and for being in solidarity with those who are
crucified with Christ still. We must seek to become the act of looking, of contemplating deeply the sorrow of God, the sorrow of this
woman-mother and all those who seek consolation and solace in
the flesh of the children of God on earth now.

We must not only learn to pray for the easing of our own sorrows
but make sure that we are not the cause of pain for others. And
then we must seek to be the one who consoles, who soothes and

brings balm and the oil of healing and gladness to others. There is an apt prayer in the Ethiopic Liturgy, a prayer that is probably from the fourth or fifth century. We pray it with this Mother of God for all who know sorrow, but especially those who know sorrow because of association with the sign of contradiction that is the Word of God made flesh:

> Holy Lord, Holy one, strong, living and immortal,
> Son of the Virgin Mary, have mercy on us!
>
> Holy Lord, Holy one, strong, living and immortal,
> baptized in the Jordan and raised up on the cross,
> have mercy on us!
>
> Holy Lord, Holy one, strong, living and immortal,
> who rose from the dead on the third day,
> and having ascended into heaven sits at the right hand of
>   the Father
> And will come again in glory to judge the living and the
>   dead,
> have mercy on us!
>
> Glory be to the Father and to the Son and to the Holy Spirit
> now and for ever through all ages.
> Amen! So be it!
> Holy Lord, living Trinity, have mercy on us!

20

Sainte Thérèse de l'Enfant-Jésus et la Sainte-Face

I desired that, like the Face of Jesus, my face be truly hidden, and that no one on earth would know me. I thirsted after suffering and I longed to be forgotten.   (Thérèse of Lisieux)

St. Thérèse is most commonly known by the name Thérèse of the Child Jesus, but she took both that name and the name Thérèse of the Holy Face for her new identity in Christ when she took her vows at Carmel. Both names, the Child and the Holy Face, span the life of Christ — he was the beloved child of God in baptism, acknowledged and publicly proclaimed by the Father in the power of the Spirit; and he was the Crucified One whose face was marred by suffering and the hate of others. The gentle little child is balanced by the strong, enduring adult child of God. Thérèse was conscious of the entirety of the gospel — from Jesus' birth through his growth in awareness of the presence and power of transforming love to the ultimate beckoning of love in sacrifice and death.

In this icon, Thérèse holds the image of the crucified and stricken face of Jesus in death close to her heart, as though attached to her scapular, her mantle that signifies her bearing of the cross of Christ, her new baptismal garment. This image is based on an actual picture that Thérèse used in her meditations and prayer.

150

Thérèse was a Carmelite, the bearer of a rich tradition of intimacy with the child and the Crucified Christ. There is a story of Carmel that is told about the great Saint Teresa of Ávila when the child appeared to her and asked, "Who are you?" She answered, "Teresa of Jesus. Who are you?" and the child answered, "Jesus of Teresa." These intimate relationships are rooted in tradition and even more deeply in the Scriptures.

It is said that Thérèse's "little way" is a simple and profound synthesis of John of the Cross's and Teresa of Ávila's own worlds of spirituality. Thérèse herself was a painter who often attempted to portray with utmost simplicity a "childlike" way, a visual image of what she sought to incorporate bodily into her life and religiously into her soul's sense of who Jesus the Christ, the Word made flesh, truly is as he dwells among us. She lived "inside" the gospel, attempting to distill the richness and depth of the Word throughout her daily life and prayer with intensity, passion, and grace. Far from being the delicate creature some have depicted her to be, she was closer to the stark reality of purgation and suffering that are core to the transfiguration of humans into the radiant face of the One in whose image we are made.

She often referred to herself as "the unpetalled rose." This image does not refer to the proud, elegant, or beautiful vision of the rose we associate with Thérèse. Instead, this rose is thrown to the wind, torn apart, devoid of meaning, except as it is undone and scattered on the ground, bits of color and texture that are completely given away in worship and honor of another. She writes in her journal:

> The unpetalled rose is the faithful image, O Divine Child,
> of the heart which wishes to immolate itself for you
> unreservedly
> at every instant.

Lord, more than a fresh rose upon your altars, loves to
    sparkle,
she gives herself to You; but I dream of something else:
to be unpetalled.

This is the devotion, the hard asceticism, of a warrior, almost in the Japanese Zen tradition. Elsewhere she calls herself "little zero," nothing by herself, saying that if it follows a numeral, a zero (as in 10) can be a help, but not if it comes before (as in 01). She speaks of "ceasing to exist" in the same lines in which she mentions "happily abandoning myself to You, Jesus." Her spirituality is solidly scriptural, referring to herself as "a grain of sand," reduced to ashes, ground down. She is echoing her Master's lines in John's gospel:

The hour has come for the Son of Man to be glorified. Amen, amen. I say to you, unless a grain of wheat falls to the ground and dies, it remains just a grain of wheat; but if it dies, it produces much fruit. Whoever loves his life loses it, and whoever hates his life in this world will preserve it for eternal life. Whoever serves me must follow me, and where I am, there also will my servant be. The Father will honor whoever serves me.

(John 12:23–26)

This young woman, a vowed Carmelite, stands securely in the tradition of those who dedicated themselves to accompanying the Crucified One, walking the way traditionally called the *via negativa* which is, paradoxically, the way to glory and revelation of the holiness of God. The verse from John quoted above continues:

"I am troubled now. Yet what should I say? 'Father, save me from this hour'? But it was for this purpose that I came to this hour. Father, glorify your name.... Now is the time of judgment on this world; now the ruler of this world will be

driven out. And when I am lifted up from the earth, I will
draw everyone to myself."   (John 12:27–28a, 31–32, NAB)

This icon has the child Jesus clinging alongside Thérèse, barefoot and clutching at her scapular. She is a young woman, perhaps
twenty years of age, and she clutches the icon of the crucified and
murdered beloved child of God, her hand cupping the face that rests
on her heart. In her other hand is the fabled rose, but unpetalled,
scattered, and falling to the ground, as homage and sacrifice, em-
blematic of her own life, given over. In one of her prayers she wrote:
"The nature of Love is to lower itself." This is the condescension
of God toward all of us, and for Thérèse, the word "Love" is a
synonym for the Incarnate Word that is God's mercy on us in Jesus.
She was intent on being a warrior, a missionary, a priest, but as she
wrote: "I am not a warrior who fights with earthly weapons but with
the 'sword of the Spirit' which is the Word of God." She prayed
constantly to see things the way they truly are, to see the truth.

The image she holds is that of the Man of Sorrows. Toward
the end of her life she said: "To surrender to another, to Jesus, is
a supremely purifying process. Suffering is born when the Sacred
Face of the Man of Sorrows casts a glance on someone. This glance
left an imprint of the Sorrowful Redeemer on the Disciple." And
she cried out in her pain that was both physical and intensified by
spiritual darkness: "I sing what I *want* to believe!" This young dying
woman sought the face of the child of God, not a young four- or
five-year-old, but the beloved child of God of Jesus' baptism: "You
are my beloved Son; with you I am well pleased" (Luke 3:22b).
This was the image of God that she called on the Spirit to imprint
upon her soul and life.

The icon of the Child and the Holy Face that Thérèse gazed
upon so intently and contemplated in her short life invites us to

take to heart the words of Jesus and meditate upon them until they become flesh of our flesh and deeply embedded in our spirits. It is a lifetime of becoming unpetalled roses, and laying down our lives following in this beloved child of God's footsteps:

> Come to me, all you who labor and are burdened, and I will give you rest. Take my yoke upon you and learn from me, for I am meek and humble of heart; and you will find rest for yourselves. For my yoke is easy, and my burden light.
>
> (Matt. 11:28–30)

In Thérèse's twenty-four years of life, the Word of God matured in her, and in the last year of her life, which was a relentless, excruciating breakdown of her body and purifying of her soul, she knew her distance from God, the darkness of doubt, and the desperate yet conscious clinging to faith in the Word made flesh. Simple as they are, her last words were: "My God, I love you." In the end, one becomes a true Doctor of the Church because of the wideness of one's love and of faith that draws one into the heart of the body of Christ and the church. The fullness of the gospel is love, the love of God the Child and the tortured Crucified One.

She could pray with the early saints of the church, as we pray using old words:

> Your presence brings courage; sweet is your exhalation
> And venerable your face, O holy God.
> Every form of life springs from you,
> You are the bread of life in the house of bread [Bethlehem]
> Because you have life from the only source of life;
> Your breath draws us gently, full of wisdom is your infancy. . . .
> O little child and yet ancient of days,
> O shepherd and yet a young lamb benign and affable![37]

21

Holy New Martyr
Sister Mary Antoinette,
Daughter of Wisdom

Wisdom is the Cross; the Cross is Wisdom.

(St. Louis de Monfort, founder of Daughters of Wisdom)

What is Wisdom? *Sophia* is the Greek word. *Hokmah* in Hebrew. *Premudrost* in Russian. All the words are grammatically feminine. In the Scriptures, Wisdom is a person, a woman, and in the Book of Proverbs she raises her voice and cries aloud in the street (1:20), exhorting and pleading for a return to the Word of God and righteousness and obedience. She is the source of truth, a hidden treasure, knowledge and understanding, a shield and guardian of justice, a source of protection. She is even imaged as the builder of a house (9:1). And in the Second Testament, Paul writes: "We proclaim Christ crucified, . . . Christ the power of God and the wisdom of God. For the foolishness of God is wiser than human wisdom, and the weakness of God is stronger than human strength" (1 Cor. 1:23–25).

In this icon, Sister Mary Antoinette, a member of the congregation of the Daughters of Wisdom, is visited by Wisdom, in the traditional form with wings of the Spirit, bearing the blood-red cross, with her hand laid on Mary Antoinette's forehead in

blessing, strengthening and imparting the gift of the Word and intimacy, the shared grace of martyrdom for the truth of the gospel. The background is that of the Congo — it is Isangi, about eighty miles northwest of Stanleyville on the Congo River, where Mary was stationed as a missionary working in a school, an orphanage, and a hospital from 1961 until her death in 1964. It was her second assignment to Africa. Mary Antoinette grasps her profession and mission cross with her own hands crossed, her right hand raised in prayer and receptivity. Her eyes are wide open and her face serene. She is dressed in her community's missionary habit.

She worked in the Congo, in her own words "not respected, but tolerated." Originally from Long Island, she entered the Daughters of Wisdom, not strictly an American order, with the words: "When I go, I intend to take both feet with me, to leave no part of me in the world." For years, she resisted asking for a mission assignment, bowing to her parents' wishes, but in 1952, at age thirty-nine, she left for her first assignment in Malawi and stayed six years. After reassignment to the States, she left again in 1961. She had written in her journal: "I want to be a martyr, but that's probably not possible. At least I want to go to the missions, to teach, to work in a hospital, even just to cook." This was her lifelong hope, intent, and desire, while she taught science, Latin, algebra, and religion. During her stay there, the Congo went through a time of unrest and violence, and she knew the danger she was in. Eventually, she was the only American who remained in the community.

The discontent, the taunts, and the hostility escalated, and in October 1964 the Isangi community was captured by the Congolese rebels. For weeks there was no word, and then the New York community was notified by the State Department that forty-four missionaries who had been missing were found alive, but two, Belgian Sister Marie Françoise and American Sister Mary Antoinette, had been killed. The rescued hostages reported that the American sister had been "subjected to degrading humiliation, beaten with rifle butts, sticks, and machetes at the foot of a monument to the late communist premier Patrice Lumumba, and her body thrown into the Congo River." She had written to her sisters: "God alone knows what will be the ending of all this chaos and strife, but whatever we do now will be a beginning."

Later her community learned from several Canadian Daughters of Wisdom who had been rescued and who were present at her death that she knew she was going to be killed. "She prepared herself by praying for strength and guidance to which she added the itinerary prayers of the Congregation customarily said by those about to embark on a trip. Rising from her knees she said to the sisters: 'This time the trip will be to heaven.'" She was martyred on November 19, 1964. She was a new martyr, born of the wisdom of the cross.

The Wisdom of God, the Logos, the Word made flesh and crucified, the Holiness of God who is a person teaches the power of weakness, of faithfulness, and of the freedom of the children of God. The wisdom of missionaries is rooted in Jesus' prayer for laborers to be sent into the fields, ripe for the harvesting. Jesus thirsts for followers, for those devoted to the will of the Father and for those who will go forth into the world, as the Father sent him to preach the gospel of human dignity, hope, and service to one another in love. Jesus tells his disciples:

My food is to do the will of the one who sent me and to finish his work. Do you not say, "In four months the harvest will be here"? I tell you, look up and see the fields ripe for the harvest. The reaper is already receiving his payment and gathering crops for eternal life, so that the sower and the reaper can rejoice together. For here the saying is verified that "One sows and another reaps." I sent you to reap what you have not worked for; others have done the work, and you are sharing the fruits of their work.   (John 4:34–38)

This mission work is not necessarily what you do or even what you say; more than anything else it is one's very presence among people. The ancient saying that "in the blood of martyrs is the seed of Christians" is the paradoxical wisdom of the seed sown and the faith of the community being strengthened in the death of its members. This Wisdom makes one the message and the messenger, and it binds one in the blood of the cross, in the power of the resurrection, in every generation and every part of the world. Baptism bears fruit in the witness to love and a life laid down freely in the face of senseless rage and destruction. The giving of life and the manner of dying speak volumes in a universal language. This is Wisdom that can only be known and understood in one's own flesh and integrated into one's soul by dying with gracefulness on the wings of the Spirit.

And then Wisdom indeed pervades and penetrates all things and Wisdom's words come true: "Lo! I will pour out to you my spirit, I will acquaint you with my words" (Prov. 1:23); "get wisdom; at the cost of all you have, get understanding. . . . She will put on your head a graceful diadem: a glorious crown will she bestow on you" (Prov. 4:7b–9). This is the martyr's crown, the priceless gift stumbled upon and sometimes given as part of the gift in the waters of baptism and dedication to the gospel.

Whether we pray for the gift of martyrdom or not, we are all called to pray for the gift of holiness and the Wisdom of God, born of water and the Spirit, a Wisdom that leads us to shout out with our lives the love of God for us in Jesus Christ All Merciful.

Together we can pray with Sister Mary Antoinette for this gift beyond compare:

> O Wisdom, come,
> anoint me with your love;
> accept my total commitment to you.
> Grant me the grace to serve with fidelity in the missions
> and the courage, if necessary, to give my life.

This simple prayer of petition to Wisdom might be bound with those of the ones who have gone before us in faith, in long-enduring and courageous witness to Love made flesh and dwelling among us. All our prayers can be made one in a hope that is everlasting, connected in a web encompassing all the world, and in missionaries that brought this Wisdom with them as they journeyed into the unknown and the dangerous places, all for love.

Closing Prayer

"Everything has been entrusted to me by my Father. No one knows the Son except the Father, and no one knows the Father except the Son and those to whom the Son chooses to reveal him."

(A prayer of Jesus from Matthew 11:27)

Holy! Holy! Holy! God Father, Son and Spirit, the Trinity of Mercy.

You are the source and sun of mercy rising in the glories of morning.

You are the depths of mercy in the midst of noonday heat.

You are mercy singing in the darkest time of night.

You are mercy within mercy within mercy.

You are the mercy of creation born out of emptiness and longing.

You are the mercy of history turning and turning.

You are the mercy of promises rainbowed in sky and prophets' words.

You are the mercy of presence in wind, fire, earth, sea, mist and moon, wood and stars.

You are the mercy of prayer, silent screaming and singing, and utter stillness.

You are Mercy born of a woman, flesh and blood and bone, a human face among us.

You are Mercy growing in wisdom, aging with grace and loving all that has been made in God's own image.

You are Mercy walking the earth, lost in the stars and partial to mountain solitudes and deserts.

You are Mercy's gentle Spirit touching the torn, hurting bodies, exhausted minds, and bent and broken hearts.

You are Mercy's wise words speaking hope, telling stories, and teaching with unbearable power.

You are Mercy's power streaked with the consolation of the anointing of the Spirit.

You are Mercy's judgment born of the knowledge and necessity of justice.

You are Mercy and Justice kissing.

You are Mercy crying out in agony: in betrayal, in loss of friends, in the ugly conspiracy of hate.

You are Mercy being butchered by torture, the death penalty, and the self-righteousness of religion.

You are Mercy laid in the earth, and earth knows its own maker.

You are Mercy kissed by Father and Spirit and raised from the dead.

You are Mercy's Spirit of forgiveness, reconciliation, amnesty, atonement whispered unceasingly.

You are Mercy, terrible and true.

We worship you Father, Son, and Spirit: Mercy-maker, Mercy-freeing, Mercy-winging Peace to all.

We worship you who wrap your merciful presences around us and hold us all ways.

Holy Holy Holy Mercy Mercy Mercy, you who are the Holy One. Make us holy. Make us Merciful.

Amen. Amen. Amen.

Notes

1. Unless otherwise noted, quotes from the Church Fathers are from Jill Haak Adels, ed., *The Wisdom of the Saints: An Anthology* (New York: Oxford University Press, 1987).

2. John Baggley, *Doors of Perception: Icons and Their Spiritual Significance* (Crestwood, N.Y.: St. Vladimir's Seminary Press, 1988), 23–24.

3. Nicholas Cabasilas, *The Life in Christ* (Crestwood, N.Y.: St. Vladimir's Seminary Press, 1974), 49–50.

4. Simone Weil, *Waiting for God* (New York: HarperCollins, 1973).

5. Symeon the New Theologian, oration 61, in *Works* (Moscow, 1892); quoted in Leonid Ouspensky, *Theology of the Icon* (Crestwood, N.Y.: St. Vladimir's Seminary Press, 1992), 1:33.

6. Quoted by Agnes Cunningham, S.S.C.M., "Jesus Christ in Eastern Christianity," *Chicago Studies* 38, no. 2 (summer/fall 1999): 142.

7. Scripture references in this introduction are from the New Revised Standard Version; Scripture references throughout the remainder of the text are from the *Christian Community Bible*.

8. Versions sung at St. Benedict's Abbey, Snowmass, Colorado.

9. "Hark! A Clarion Voice Is Sounding" (Vox clara ecce intonat), tenth century, trans. Edward Caswall (1849), in *Trappist Hymnal for Advent/Christmas.*

10. David M. Denny, "Roots"; quoted in *Desert Call,* a magazine published by the Spiritual Life Institute, in Colorado.

11. William Hart McNichols, S.J. We should remember that an icon is written, not painted, because it is the text of Scripture told or actualized in a liturgical-sacramental presence. The icon makes past and present reality simultaneous.

12. Evelyn Underhill, quoted in *The Plough Reader* (autumn 2001): 24.

13. "The Paradise That Is within the Cave," in John Balley, *Festival Icons for the Christian Year* (London: Mowbrays, 2000), 131.

14. *Corde natus ex Parentis,* 413 A.D.

15. Excerpts from Eberhard Arnold, ed., *The Early Christians* (Farmington, Pa.: Plough Publishing, 1998), 46.

16. In James Brockman, ed., *The Violence of Love* (Farmington, Pa.: Plough, 1998).

17. Cited by Francis W. Johnston, *Heart of the Saints* (London: T. Shand Publications, 1975).

18. Dorothy Day, *Meditations* (Baltimore: Newman Press, 1970).

19. Letter to Pope Gregory XI, in Adels, ed., *Wisdom of the Saints.*

20. Tom Cowan, *The Way of the Saints: Prayers, Practices, and Meditations* (New York: Putnam, 1998).

21. Cyril of Jerusalem, in *The Wisdom of the Saints: Anthology,* ed. Jill Haak Adels (New York: Oxford University Press, 1987).

22. In James Brockman, ed., *The Violence of Love* (Farmington, Pa.: Plough, 1998).

23. Ibid.

24. Audre Lorde, "Poetry Is Not a Luxury," in *Sister Outsider* (Freedom, Calif.: Crossing Press, 1984).

25. C. K. Williams, in Art Institute of Chicago, *Transforming Vision: Writers on Art* (Boston: Little, Brown and Co., 1994).

26. Josefa Menéndez, quoted in José de Vinck, *Revelations of Women Mystics* (Staten Island, N.Y.: Alba House, 1985), 103.

27. Quoted in the "The Living Spirit," *The Tablet* (2000): 496.

28. Note for John 19:31.

29. John Baggley, *Doors of Perception: Icons and Their Spiritual Significance* (Crestwood, N.Y.: St. Vladimir's Seminary Press, 1988), 7.

30. Agnes Cunningham, "Jesus Christ in Eastern Christianity," *Chicago Studies* 30, no. 2 (summer/fall 1999): 144–45.

31. Frank Kacmarcik and Paul Philbert, *Seeing and Believing: Images of Christian Faith* (Collegeville, Minn.: Liturgical Press, 1995), 96.

32. Daniel Berrigan, *Sorrow Built a Bridge: Friendship and AIDS* (Baltimore: Fortkamp, 1989).

33. Miriam Makeba, "My Story," *Essence* (May 1988).

34. Cited in Vincent J. Romano, "Jesus the Nonviolent Revolutionary," *Maryknoll* (March 2001): 13.

35. Quoted in "This Miracle . . . Has Changed Humanity's Destiny," from *ZENIT News Agency—The World Seen from Rome.*

36. Quoted in John Anthony McGuckin, *Standing in God's Holy Fire: The Byzantine Tradition* (Maryknoll, N.Y.: Orbis Books, 2001), 62.

37. From Constante Berselli, ed., *To Him Be Praise: Hymns to Christ in the First Millennium of the Church* (Middlegreen, England: St. Paul Productions, 1982), 65–66.

Bibliography

On Icons

Baggley, John. *Doors of Perception: Icons and Their Spiritual Significance.* Crestwood, N.Y.: St. Vladimir's Seminary Press, 1988.

————. *Festival Icons for the Christian Year.* London: Mowbrays, 2000.

Berselli, Constante, ed. *To Him Be Praise: Hymns to Christ in the First Millennium of the Church.* Middlegreen, England: St. Paul Productions, 1982.

Cavarnos, Constantine. *The Icon: Its Spiritual Basis and Purpose.* Belmont, Mass.: Institute for Byzantine and Modern Greek Studies, 1973.

Florensky, Pavel. *Iconostasis.* Crestwood, N.Y.: St. Vladimir's Seminary Press, 1996.

John of Damascus, St. *On the Divine Images.* Crestwood, N.Y.: St. Vladimir's Seminary Press, 1987.

McGuckin, John Anthony. *Standing in God's Holy Fire: The Byzantine Tradition.* Maryknoll, N.Y.: Orbis Books, 2001.

News, Solrunn. *The Mystical Language of Icons.* London: St. Paul's Publications, 2000.

Ouspensky, Leonid. *Theology of the Icon,* Vol. 1. Crestwood, N.Y.: St. Vladimir's Seminary Press, 1992.

Quenot, Michel. *The Resurrection and the Icon.* Crestwood, N.Y.: St. Vladimir's Seminary Press, 1997.

Tavener, John, and Mother Thekla. *Ikons: Meditations in Words and Music.* London: Fount, HarperCollins, 1994.

Vermes, Geza. *The Changing Faces of Jesus.* London: Penguin Press, 2000.

Ware, Kallistos. *The Orthodox Way.* London: Mowbrays, 1979.

On Jesus and Christology

Bonino, José Míguez, ed. *Faces of Jesus: Latin American Christologies.* Maryknoll, N.Y.: Orbis Books, 1984.

Brown, Raymond E., S.S. *Jesus: God and Man.* New York: Macmillan, 1967.

Burrows, Ruth. *To Believe in Jesus.* Denville, N.J.: Dimension Books, 1978.

Bussmann, Claus. *Who Do You Say? Jesus Christ in Latin American Theology.* Maryknoll, N.Y.: Orbis Books, 1985.

Chilton, Bruce. *Rabbi Jesus: An Intimate Biography: The Jewish Life and Teaching That Inspired Christianity.* New York: Doubleday, 2000.

Dupuis, Jacques, S.J. *Who Do You Say That I Am? Introduction to Christology*. Maryknoll, N.Y.: Orbis Books, 1994.

Fuller, Reginald H., and Pheme Perkins. *Who Is This Christ? Gospel Christology and Contemporary Faith*. Philadelphia: Fortress Press, 1983.

Goergen, Donald J., O.P. *Jesus, Son of God, Son of Mary, Immanuel*. Collegeville, Minn.: Liturgical Press, 1995.

Hellwig, Monika K. *Jesus: The Compassion of God*. Wilmington, Del.: Michael Glazier, 1983.

Johnson, Elizabeth. *Consider Jesus: Waves of Renewal in Christology*. New York: Crossroad, 1990.

McDermott, Brian O. *Word Become Flesh: Dimensions of Christology*. Collegeville, Minn.: Liturgical Press, 1993.

Nolan, Albert. *Jesus before Christianity*. Maryknoll, N.Y.: Orbis Books, 1996.

Schreiter, Robert J., ed. *Faces of Jesus in Africa*. Maryknoll, N.Y.: Orbis Books, 1991.

On the Early Church and Writers on Art

Adels, Jill Haak, ed. *The Wisdom of the Saints: An Anthology*. New York: Oxford University Press, 1987.

Art Institute of Chicago. *Transforming Vision: Writers on Art*. Boston: Little, Brown and Co., 1994.